The Great British Entrepreneur's Handbook 2015

Every owner of a physical copy of

The Great British Entrepreneur's Handbook 2015

can download the eBook for free direct from us at Harriman House, in a DRM-free format that can be read on any eReader, tablet or smartphone.

Simply head to:

ebooks.harriman-house.com/greatbritish15

to get your copy now.

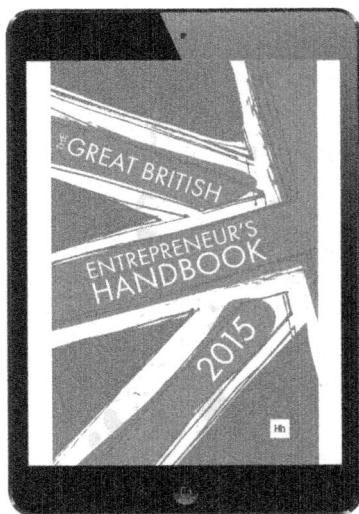

The Great British Entrepreneur's Handbook 2015

HARRIMAN HOUSE LTD
18 College Street
Petersfield
Hampshire
GU31 4AD
GREAT BRITAIN
Tel: +44 (0)1730 233870

Email: contact@harriman-house.com
Website: www.harriman-house.com

First published in Great Britain in 2014.
Each chapter remains copyright © of the respective author.

The right of the authors to be identified as the Authors has been asserted in accordance with the Copyright, Designs and Patents Act 1988.

ISBN: 9780857194381

British Library Cataloguing in Publication Data
A CIP catalogue record for this book can be obtained from the British Library.

Hh Harriman House

Contents

Foreword   1

The Great British Entrepreneur Awards
by Ian Cowie   2

Telling Your Business's Story
by Simon Burton   7

Building Bigger, Better Businesses
by Duncan Cheatle   13

The Changing Needs of Those in the Middle
by Robert Craven   19

Ten Top PR Tips
by Peter Ibbetson   25

The Psychology of Business Success
by Michael Jacobsen   31

Keeping Culture, Purpose and Values at the Heart of Your Business
by Jill Miller   37

From IP to Credible Business
by David Patterson   43

Steps to Success
by Ami Shpiro   48

Why Social Media is Good for Business
by Nick James   54

Crowdfunding
by Henry Catchpole   57

Leading Your Small Business Effectively
by Ksenia Zheltoukhova   61

SEO Made Easy
by Ann Stanley   67

A Passion to Help Others
by Karen Betts — 74

How to Win a Pitch
by Sarah Shields — 79

The Importance of Niche
by Liz Doogan-Hobbs MBE — 82

Creating and Maintaining Momentum
by Stephen Fear — 87

All About IT
by Andy Hinxman — 92

How To Go Global
by FedEx — 97

Building Your Personal Brand
by Jessica Huie MBE — 103

The Business Case for International Trade
by Samuel Kasumu and Elizabeth Adeniran — 108

Paperless – or Just Smarter Printing?
by John Gifford — 114

Plan to Get Lucky?
by Paul Samrah — 120

Improving Our Lives
by Craig Goldblatt — 127

Sponsors — **131**
NatWest — 132
MINI — 133
AXA Business Insurance — 134
Croner — 135
Dell — 136
Exact Online — 137
FedEx — 138
Friendly Pensions — 139
Kaspersky Lab — 140
Kingston Smith — 141
OKI Systems — 142
XLN — 143

Foreword

Entrepreneurs by definition make a difference. Their mindset is to confront received wisdom and find new ways of doing things. They don't take 'no' for an answer; from themselves or from others. They see old problems in new ways and in turn re-imagine, innovate and disrupt.

But there is no such thing as a standard entrepreneur road-map to entrepreneurial success. Every entrepreneur is unique and every entrepreneur's journey is different. The Great British Entrepreneur Awards celebrate entrepreneurial success in its myriad forms with the aim of inspiring more people to rise to the entrepreneurial challenge.

The Great British Entrepreneur's Handbook 2015 serves a similar but broader purpose. Its role is not simply to inspire but to guide and encourage. Its contributors represent some of the most interesting thinkers and practitioners in business today. But the handbook is not a 'how to' or an instruction manual. It's more like a tasting menu of entrepreneurial thoughts and ideas, designed to whet the appetite, provide a moment of insight or a way of navigating a challenge.

If it motivates one entrepreneur to start their journey or helps another through a sticky patch it will have done its job.

The Great British Entrepreneur Awards

by Ian Cowie

Chairman, SME banking at RBS/NatWest

This year's entries, demonstrating both the tremendous quality and the importance of UK entrepreneurs, are in. In fact, as you read this, they will have been announced.

But what actually is an entrepreneur and how do they make the world a better place?

Entrepreneurs come from a variety of backgrounds: some are products-people, others more finance-focused; they can be salespeople, programmers, or just people with a vision. But the one thing that all great entrepreneurs have in common is a desire to change things for the better: they are innovators and, because of this, they have a huge impact on the world we live in.

"We believe that entrepreneurs are the engine room of the economy, the drivers of national wealth," says Simon Burton, founder of the Great British Entrepreneur Awards. "More importantly," he adds, "we believe that entrepreneurs forge innovation, disrupt tired markets, and foster positive change."

Julie Deane, founder of the Cambridge Satchel Company, won Great British Entrepreneur of the Year in 2013. She's become an inspiration for entrepreneurs across the country by creating a business that exports to 110 countries and has had a big impact on fashion and trends across the world. Deane was rendered speechless when she won the award, but later said: "I couldn't think of a better honour."

Founder of Naked Wines, Rowan Gormley (who shares some insights on his start-up's success below) is another former winner. Gormley's business now generates revenues in excess of £50m per year. The publicity and recognition fostered by the award, he says, was tremendously beneficial.

"For a small company, it was fantastic. It really helped put us on the map and it was great that people recognised the business as something special," says Gormley.

The night itself is an emotional affair for many, and also a chance for entrepreneurs to recognise the hard work their teams have put in.

"It means a great deal; we've had a real hard slog over the last two years and this award is a real testament to our team's hard work," said Captify founders, Dominic Joseph and Adam Ludwin, who won Young Entrepreneur of the Year in 2013.

"It's lovely, when you're so caught up in the everyday running of your business," says founder of Bluebella, Emily Bendell, who won Most Captivating Entrepreneur of the Year in 2013. "Nights like tonight are a great opportunity to take the team out and enjoy the success."

British entrepreneurship is as impressive as ever, so choosing 2014's winner has been a tough task. However, Simon Burton relished the challenge.

"The entries to the Great British Entrepreneur Awards this year were inspiring and humbling," says Burton. "We passionately promote the idea that entrepreneurs' stories are as telling as their balance sheets, and that entrepreneurs should be acknowledged and recognised. The task for the judges this year was incredibly hard. Entrepreneurship is alive, thriving and blossoming in the UK."

Naked Wines: creating a new blend

Great British Entrepreneur winner Rowan Gormley describes how he created an innovative £50m business in an industry used to doing things the old way. Great businesses are often started in recessions and Naked Wines is one more for the list. However, its birth wasn't exactly planned.

"I got fired," laughs founder Rowan Gormley. "It was the best thing that ever happened to me."

Gormley had previously worked at Virgin Wines, which was subsequently taken over by Laithwaite's. However, he fell out with his new bosses and was shown the door.

"After about three months we had a disagreement and they chucked me out. But 17 other staff members chose to leave with me, and we started a new wine company." But this was 2008 and the world, says Gormley, was a crazy place. "The only way to bring anything to market was to help with the finance and selling."

Educated near the wine growing landscapes of Cape Town, South Africa, wine has always been a passion for Gormley. He saw the potential for the internet as a marketplace and believed he could use it to disrupt the winemaking industry for the good of those employed in it.

"I always thought there was something wrong with the wine business. Many firms are making a lot of money, but the farmers and winemakers hardly have enough to make a living. Many of them want to produce their own wines, but don't have the skills to sell them," Gormley says.

Seeing everything

Naked Wines creates funding for unknown winemakers to produce new types of wines and then to sell them online. The investors put £20 a month into a fund and then receive discounted wine when it's made. The winemakers get a share in the profits and their costs covered, and Naked Wines acts as the platform for it all to happen.

"We are more like Facebook than a wine company. We are a platform and tool for winemakers," Gormley explains.

It's a strategy that has worked. The company started using crowdfunding before the term even existed and now, according to Gormley, has "235,000 angel investors and a list of 10,000 waiting to join". However, this type of arrangement involves a lot of trust from all parties.

"The reason we called ourselves Naked was because we realised that people weren't going to put up money for wine they hadn't tasted and made by people they didn't know, unless there was total transparency. People needed to see everything – we *had* to be naked," he says.

Talent

A big part of the success of Naked Wines is its ability to seek out talent in the industry and bring these people to the attention of the public. This involves searching around wine regions, ignoring headline names and going off the beaten track.

"If you think about the big names, they are often attached to a chateau. You have to look behind that to find the real winemaker with the real talent," says Gormley.

Once the talent has been located, the ideas work begins and then a proposal is put forward to the online community to see if it will gain backing. Gormley says that not all winemakers like to do this. Some don't speak English, but most can overcome their fears and engage with an audience that is equally passionate about wine.

"A lot of winemakers want to make their own wines but don't have the selling skills," he explains. "These are people who are often more comfortable in the cellar than standing on a stage talking to people – but they are happy talking about wine."

Feedback

A lot of discussions take place across the company's forums and social media channels. Gormley says this is all part of the business's transparent approach and is vital to its work.

"There's a lot of openness with the customers, a lot of conversations. We don't delete bad reviews. I think if people come on the site and see good and bad reviews they will believe them."

It was when reading the online reviews during the first year of the business that Gormley realised the plan was working. One of his winemakers went on to the site and apologised that his wine hadn't been as good as he had hoped. He said there had been bad weather and his grapes had been affected. However, the reaction from investors was still supportive.

"All of our customers wrote to him and said 'Don't worry, we'll stick with you' – I realised then that this was something really different going on."

Staff

The business, which was founded in Norwich, now also has offices in Napa Valley, California, and Sydney, Australia, while its winemakers are in 13 countries. Gormley says that managing such an operation can be tough.

"It has been hard growing from a small company in Norwich to becoming one working on three continents. We work in different time zones, so the phone starts ringing at 6am and keeps going until midnight – it's always working hours somewhere."

The business now employs 160 people and has had to beef up its management team to deal with growth. However, Gormley is someone who employs on attitude rather than qualifications.

"A lot of my staff are young people who don't have university degrees or degrees geared specifically to work in the wine industry. My sales director in Australia joined after his school grades were so bad he couldn't get into university."

Future

Naked Wines is now selling over ten million bottles annually and in its last financial year generated revenues of over £50m. It's currently involved in a fine wine project for which investors have raised a £5m bond. Gormley says his future plans are more of the same and that he is far from finished with disrupting the industry.

"I want to grow bigger, but the thing that excites me more is the chance to give the wine industry a kick up the backside."

Telling Your Business's Story

by Simon Burton

*Founder of the Great British Entrepreneur Awards and
serial event and social media entrepreneur*

We live in an age of information overload. Every day we are presented with more information than faced a 16th-century peasant farmer in his lifetime. The irony, of course, is that we remain hungry for more. But how to know what to consume and what to decline?

Everyone around us faces the same dilemma every second of every day. So when we present ourselves, our projects and our enterprises to people we need to ensure our story is compelling and appetising. The narrative needs to be coherent, the characters engaging and the outcomes emotionally rewarding. And we need to do all of that in less time and with more distractions than ever before.

This is the age of the elevator pitch. Your story needs to get you and your travelling companions as quickly as possible between start and destination, we no longer have the time or appetite for epics. Beowulf and the Hydra's teeth belong to a bygone age – this is the age of the soundbite.

I used to work with a colleague who said that our company elevator pitch needed a very tall building and a very slow elevator. What he never mentioned (or seemed to notice), was that it also needed a very patient audience. He had a stubborn refusal to cut any of the elements so the story went back into the mists of time to find its beginning and meandered through all sorts of irrelevant side plots, digressions and twists that didn't get our audience (the people we should have cared about) any nearer the conclusion. Such a shame because the 'slow elevator, tall-building' opening is a strong one. But our actual delivery should have confounded the notion, not endorsed it. We weren't sitting around a campfire waiting through the night for the hunting party to return.

I'm a passionate believer in the power of entrepreneurs' stories to inspire, enthuse and energise. Entrepreneurs' stories are more important than their balance sheets. There is no £ value that can be placed on a tale that inspires others to entrepreneurial endeavour. But entrepreneurs do inspire, and they do promote positive change. One of the challenges for many modern entrepreneurs is that they don't know how to tell their own story. The standard entrepreneur myth is easy to construct and deliver, so too often the stories are standardised – and they fail to inspire and fail to soar.

Too many entrepreneurs fall back on cliché and tired story lines to tell their tale. As a result they end up underselling themselves, their business and their hard-work. As a rule I don't have a problem with clichés. They are clichés because of repetition and they are repeated because they contain a truth. But too often the cliché means we don't hear the truth, just the formula.

The typical entrepreneur success story runs something like this:

'I always struggled at school and I was repeatedly told I would never amount to much. Sometimes I went to university. I started work. My job was totally boring and I was completely unfulfilled. Every day I drove to work past an amazing (insert material object here – it's usually a car) and wondered how I would ever possess such a thing and how I could quit my boring job.

'One day as I was working at my boring job I had an amazing idea for (insert amazing idea here). It vaguely related to a hobby/passion/ interest of mine. I quit my boring job to pursue my dream even though everyone including my mum/except my mum told me not to. I invested everything in the business and ended up sleeping on a friend's sofa. In spite of the amazing idea and my Herculean labours the business struggled.

'I was about to give up and go back to the aforementioned boring job or a very similar and equally boring alternative job, dependent on how aggressively I had quit the first one, when a stranger quite literally mysterious in some way, came into the story for no apparent reason and presented me with a contract, large investment, way of tweaking my idea to make it successful.

'The business grew unbelievably quickly (like a magic beanstalk) and I had to recruit lots of people to work for me. I made sure, however, that everyone loved their jobs and work was never boring. We were very successful, but it was hard work and even though I now had my own bed in my own house I never saw it because I was working so hard.

'A big corporation, but not one of the evil ones I had been fighting against all along, a nice fluffy one who made work wonderful for all employees, offered me a large chest of treasure to sell them my business. Now I drive the car/boat/helicopter/tank that I coveted all those years ago and I live happily ever after telling my tale to one and all in between finally sleeping in my own giant comfy bed.'

This narrative fails for two reasons. It turns the story into the simple pre-determinism of a fairy story. There's nothing inherently wrong with fairy stories, as we'll see shortly, but old-school fairy-tales are predictable and so lack emotional punch. We know how they are going to end so we lose interest in the journey. Plus we tend to see them unravelling without any great effort on the part of the hero/heroine; circumstances and magic drive them forward as much as ingenuity and insight, so the outcome seems more lottery win and less fruits of hard-work and endeavour.

There is a reason that fairy tales, myths and legends have endured for so long. Stories and sharing those stories is fundamental to what it means to be human. Many of the great myths are common across cultures, and the components and building blocks of story-telling are universal. As indeed are the concept, character and challenges the hero faces. There's a standard path to the narrative of all heroes, from Hercules to Robin Hood, Cinderella to Alice in Wonderland, Dorothy to Luke and Buzz Lightyear to Emmet.

The basic way of telling a story is hardwired into human DNA so everyone, even those raised by wolves, is able to do the basics. And you can see the basics in every story everywhere: literary novels, soap operas, gangster movies, comic books, video games, broadsheet newspapers, trashy magazines.

With a few tweaks here and there, the basic structure looks something like this:

- humble beginnings

- grand ideas that are beaten down

- constant desire to see things in a new light

- challenges from evil empires and vested interests

- resilience in the face of adversity

- problem solving and imagination

- new ways of doing things

- trusted companions, partners and mentors

- at the moment of despair, success

- happiness and fulfilment but at a price/lessons learned.

It's a structure that is everywhere and everyone can tell a story that matches the structure. But that doesn't mean that it's easy; the truth is that effective story-telling is in itself a labour worthy of a hero.

The first challenge is the same as for every task we can all do. Just because we can all do it, doesn't mean we can all do it equally *well*. Some people are more gifted and talented as story-tellers than others. Some people practise harder, get expert training, solicit feedback and self-critique. There is an art to story-telling – it's art, and it's an art that everyone can and should get better at. But because it's so personal we tend not to tell people the truth. Story-telling – like its sister, presenting to an audience – can fill many with dread. And because it's a dread, we tend to sugar-coat the pill of any feedback we get, confusing support and encouragement with helpful critique and analysis. To get better we really need insightful comments and thoughts about our performance.

Because … it's not all about the narrator. Every audience (and every audience member) is different. Just because the basic structure is common doesn't mean our tastes, world views and experiences are shared. The very best story-tellers adapt and shape their narrative, lexicon, tone and pace to suit each audience. It's also essential to match these elements to the environment: coffee shop, board meeting, investor presentation, client pitch, bank manager all require a deftness of tongue and quickness of mind to ensure your story and environment are in harmony.

And finally, the big challenge. We're not just overwhelmed by information in the modern world, we're overwhelmed by high-quality, well-presented information. We're used to imaginative narrative structures, compelling characters, succinct story-lines, external references, flashbacks, witty asides and endings that surprise and delight – all the while confirming to our hardwired ideas. **This is not an age in which you can tell a dated story.** Or rather, you can tell a dated story, but you have to tell it in a modern fashion.

Audiences simply won't put up with being bored. Why should they, when there is something interesting just over there? Think of yourself as the audience and pick your own examples, watch your favourite contemporary TV show and then watch the show that was your favourite in a similar genre ten years ago. Do it properly, take off the rose-tinted spectacles of nostalgia. The new show isn't necessarily better, it isn't necessarily more relevant, but (and of course the exceptions do prove the rule here) it is more contemporary and will resonate more.

We all get 'once upon a time' and 'happily ever after'. We all get rags to riches, we all get the triumph of the underdog. But in a world drowning in data and bursting with information, the old ways of telling stories simply won't cut it. Far too many entrepreneurs tell their stories with the timbre and metre of the past. They lack pace, they lack drama, they lack characterisation and they lack wit and in telling their stories thus these entrepreneurs do themselves great disservice.

This is a shame, because **the entrepreneur's journey is the hero's journey.** In our modern world of business, social and environmental challenges, entrepreneurs are the heroes. They are the centre of the action, the saviours of the consumer, the champions of innovation, the pursuers of success, the instigators of purpose, the creators of national wealth. In a world short of dragons and hydras there are still plenty of real world demons that the entrepreneur hero can defend us from.

The etymology of the words hero and heroine is linked to 'defender' and 'protector', but what seems more interesting to me is the sense of a hero as *doer*, a person of action, a force of energy and strength of will. Heroes undertake labours, they protect the weak from abuses of power, they build teams, they use their skills and talents with purpose, they attack tasks that others deem impossible, they change the world for good. In short, they get stuff done.

The hero's journey is the entrepreneur's journey. Now is the time for entrepreneurs to tell their tales.

Selling yourself and your idea to investors, elevator pitches at networking events, engaging with partners, presenting to prospective clients and of course exciting purchasers when it's time to exit the business mean that never before has the story-telling skill been so important in the entrepreneur's armoury.

The journey might be full of twists and turns, but now is the time to get your story straight.

Building Bigger, Better Businesses

by Duncan Cheatle

Founder of Prelude Group

Only one in 20,000 of us builds a business to 250 staff or more – why and what do they know that most of us don't?

The UK now has five times the number of businesses than in the 1970s, when we had fewer than a million. Last year alone, Brits created more than half a million new businesses. I'm proud to have played a small part in this record level of business creation through my involvement as co-founder of StartUp Britain (a private sector funded campaign launched by the prime minister in 2011) and as non-exec and now advisory board member of the Start Up Loans Company (a government-funded programme that has provided over 20,000 mentor-supported loans to start-up entrepreneurs).

The number of larger businesses is actually falling

But this increased rate of business creation hides a more worrying fact. Of the five million businesses in the UK, three quarters have no staff at all and only 5% have more than ten. Why does this matter? Because whilst we are seeing more businesses start (and inevitably fail), we are also seeing fewer grow to a significant size. Indeed the number of businesses with more than 250 staff has actually fallen by nearly 10% since the turn of the century to around just 6,600!

In other words, by the time you take out the long established FTSE businesses and corporate-run private businesses I'd estimate that only around one in 20,000 of UK businesses has what it takes to scale to this size. If you include all those that build medium-sized businesses (50 staff plus) we are still only talking about fewer than 40,000 businesses or 1 in 1,500 of the business population.

So what do those very small number of founders do that almost all others fail to do?

Well, over the last ten years I've had the good fortune to chair over 500 round tables at The Supper Club (home to more than 300 of Britain's fastest-growing business owners) and here are eight things I have noticed over the years that most of us do *not* do (or are not even aware of) but which the most successful obsess about...

1. Have a clear mission

We are all keen to build a talented, highly-motivated team with low staff turnover, which delivers high quality output consistently and efficiently. But how do you attract and keep such talent?

When we start a business we normally have an idea of where we'd like to end up. It's this dream and the passion to deliver it that helps us, against the odds, to attract our first members of staff. Of course, the original plan normally changes, but for most of us we also lose sight of this vision as the day-to-day pressures build up. And in doing so we give up one of our natural advantages in attracting and retaining talent.

How many founders can honestly say that they would get consistent answers if they asked every one of their team what they felt was the long-term plan for the business? Very few, I suspect.

The point is that if we don't have a clear, believable and correctly understood vision for our business, why should anyone with any real talent come and work for us – assuming we aren't paying significantly more than our larger, better-known competitors just down the road? The best businesses repeat and communicate their vision at every opportunity. They also make them big and bold. Great talent is attracted to an ambitious business, one with a clear purpose.

As Simon Sinek so engagingly put it in his TED talk, successful businesses and people start with the 'why?' rather than the 'what?' A business should have a mission.

2. Work to values not rules

Likewise, sharing what values drive your business is also a very effective way of attracting and filtering staff and can prove a very effective way of communicating how we do business inside and outside our businesses.

Also, if really embraced, a values-driven business can largely dispense with rules. It is almost impossible to come up with rules for every eventuality and this approach dehumanises the workplace. Again we have to ask ourselves why great talent would want to work in such a rules-based environment over one that allows freedom within broader principles.

3. Less is more

Many entrepreneurs are easily distracted by shiny new projects, which end up diffusing energy and resources. I have never seen a first-time entrepreneur scale really fast-running multiple businesses. A portfolio approach is possible once we have made our first fortune and can attract strong management teams from the outset.

When it comes to effective communication, less is more. Effective advertising copy is short for a reason. The best businesses keep things simple, consistent and brief. And wherever possible they make messages highly visible and visual.

As Mark Twain famously said, "I didn't have time to write you a short letter so I wrote a long one instead". A 60-page business plan is one that may be useful as a tool for collecting our thoughts but is useless as a communication tool. The best businesses I've seen find a way of summarising their vision and the plan to achieve it on one page. And then put it up for all to see.

Procter & Gamble famously insist on internal notes being one-page only. This takes time and effort on the part of those creating it but saves time for recipients and ensures messages don't get lost in translation. The best businesses eliminate ambiguity.

Time invested up front in getting communications right is rewarded down the line.

4. Diseconomies of scale

Most people have heard of and understand the principle of economies of scale and for the most part people believe this to apply to their business, when in fact the reverse is almost certainly true. The vast majority of start-ups face **diseconomies of scale**. Most of us start a business from home, needing to provide a net income for ourselves alone. As soon as we take on a member of staff, we have a step cost to accommodate even if we do spread the workload. Very quickly we need to move into offices with all the associated costs. When we get to a certain size we need to start hiring managers to help coordinate the team, another step cost. And so on …

Now, couple the fact that inflation increases our cost base over time and most of us are naturally hesitant to price up and it's no wonder we see decreasing net margins as we grow sales.

The businesses that survive and thrive combine growth with improved margins. In other words they not only expand their customer base and the amount they sell but also find ways to price up, reduce costs and improve productivity through better people, processes and use of technology.

A relentless focus on margin as well as top line is vital, which is why I often say that if 'cash is king', margin is emperor!

5. The time trap

Of our limited resources, time is perhaps the most precious, as it can't be bought and can't be expanded or extended. The clock ticks relentlessly.

The most prevalent setback I witness amongst business owners who fail to scale is an inability to manage time effectively: to focus on the right things at the right time in the business. They typically get stuck very quickly at the coal face, focused on the daily challenges of business. As a result they can't see what's coming: the opportunities *or* the threats. They make themselves indispensable. They have fallen into what I call the 'time trap'. This is perhaps the biggest own goal any business owner can make.

The result of this is an ambition to scale that never matches reality. The business becomes a commitment and chore rather than a joy and a vehicle to wealth or financial independence.

The question we should all ask ourselves is: could I take a three month break from my business with no significant consequences? If the answer's no, then the next question is why? Is it because I can't let go, I don't have capable enough staff? What can I do to remedy this?

6. Become redundant

The best entrepreneurs avoid the time trap by recognising from the start that they can't scale a business without finding and keeping people better than themselves in core roles. They typically follow two basic steps:

- **Step 1** – is to focus on what they do best (sales, product development or whatever). Delegate the rest. If cash is tight, hire part-time people (FDs, etc). If the hires don't work out, don't give up on this; try again until you get it right.

- **Step 2** – is to make themselves redundant. In effect they look to remove themselves from the day to day as quickly as they can so that they can focus on the future, the big picture and building the ideal team and business.

Neil Berkett, ex-CEO of Virgin Media, very aptly described his job as CEO as being about everything beyond three months. Anything less than that was his management team's responsibility.

The old adage of working on the business not in the business could not be more true!

7. Learn from others

We all hopefully learn from our mistakes, but the best know that learning from the mistakes of others is a lot less costly. I'm always staggered when I hear people don't have time to seek out others and learn from them. The correlation between those who scale a business successfully and those who take time out of their business to learn from mentors and peers and to invest in their own development is marked.

Imagine being part of a peer group where you learn vicariously each month about the good, the bad and the ugly in a variety of other fast-growing businesses. It's gold dust. Working all hours on the wrong things is being a busy fool.

8. Manage risk and build capital value

History tells us, sadly, that businesses do not survive indefinitely. The key is to keep an eye on what might deal a fatal blow and adapt quickly to market changes.

If you ran one of the major web analytics businesses back in 2004 you'd probably feel like you were on the road to millions with a probable IPO or trade exit just around the corner. I imagine it was more than a shock to Webtrends and other market leaders when Google bought Urchin Software and then proceeded to give away Google Analytics for free!

Different sectors clearly have different risk profiles, but it's not just technology that gets hit: almost all sectors are affected by market or regulatory changes, from financial services to online retail's assault on the high street. Some are more sudden than others, but the message should be the same – we all need a contingency plan.

The most successful entrepreneurs build capital value from the start. We should all aim to build a business that others would buy for the very good reason that circumstances can change and one day we may need to sell the business. What good is our life's work if it won't function without us and nobody will buy it?

The Changing Needs of Those in the Middle

by Robert Craven

Bestselling business author and speaker, founder of The Directors' Centre

The business development needs of small and large businesses seem to be catered for by coaches and big-ticket consultancies, respectively. However, the market is failing to satisfy the needs of the directors of *medium*-sized businesses. This is a failure in terms of 1) not giving clients what they really want and need, and 2) missing opportunities to deliver consultancy that adds true value to the businesses of clients.

What's available to help the growing business is limited and inappropriate for the real needs of clients. Recent surveys and reports confirm that consulting firms and the business support industry as a whole are failing to deliver what growing entrepreneurial businesses really need.

FACT: the guru-based model of expert advice may not give the client what the client really needs

The recent fad for guru-based, personality-based consulting firms may have now peaked. There are now many, probably *too* many, so-called gurus. Or at least too many people claiming to be or being accredited as gurus.

While years ago there were successful-business-folk-turned-gurus, today there are salesmen-turned-gurus. By adopting Americanised direct marketing and presentational practices, they have become predators on the ignorant and unwary. This loss of quality and growth in quantity has been exacerbated by the recession-driven burgeoning of the coaches market: thousands of coaches offering competitively-priced (=cheap?) services to low-grade companies with little growth potential.

All of this has devalued 'guruship', especially in the eyes of prime, middle-market directors.

While accepting that the principles promoted by many gurus are well-founded and well-presented, the results achieved for most companies are not sustainable. Too many gurus offer too-good-to-be-true silver bullets.

However, it needs to be said that there *are* routes to success, that there are *some* certainties of outcome, that there are methodologies to be adopted, and strategies to be identified, which *do* work, and these can be implemented by many companies.

FACT: Guru-led consultancy practices create a schizophrenic proposition

The get-rich-quick, too-good-to-be-true propositions 'work' for those clients who are ignorant, inexperienced, desperate, or all three. However, they do not resonate with experienced business people (the middle market); they know they need help, but they don't believe in miracles. It is no surprise, then, that the vast majority of guru fodder are companies that are very small (or very large).

FACT: Hard things are hard

Most business books and their authors attempt to provide recipes for challenges that have no recipes. There is rarely a recipe for a really complicated, dynamic situation. And most situations are not straightforward. "The hard thing about hard things is that there is no formula for dealing with them," in the words of Ben Horowitz.

QUESTION: Is there a middle ground? A third way?

Between the siren calls of the gurus and the leaden drone of certain academics lies a sweet spot that can really appeal to experienced business people. It combines the practical methodologies of the gurus with the intelligent, analytical skills of the academics. It promises results – but not miracles or degrees. It is neither quick nor slow, cheap nor expensive.

FACT or OPINION?: Guru/coaching fails small businesses

Here is one version of what is going on. This is perfectly simple: guru/coaching is *how-to*. It isn't where, when, how, who, how much, or with what result. It does not address the real problems most small/new businesses have. The smaller clients do not know what direction they should be going in – or are not sure about it; their biggest challenge is therefore strategic (where they should be going) and not tactical (how they should get there).

How-to gurus/coaches help clients get further down the road they are on. And faster. They don't usually do more than cursorily check if that is the right or best road for that particular business in its market, or with its management strengths and weaknesses.

OPINION: At the opposite extreme ...

While gurus/coaches are happy to work (metaphorically) for a good dinner, heavyweight management consultants want signature rights to your bank account. Where gurus/coaches work from the inside (and rarely see the big wide world), management consultants start on the outside, and work their way in.

They say they can't talk about your business without understanding the world and local economies, your market, its trends, its leaders, its dynamics. Then they need to understand your company inside out – interviews, research etc. with staff, then all over again with clients, suppliers etc. Then they need to work out the strategy for your business. Then how to implement that strategy. Then they need to hold your hand while you do it.

This is big ticket, big commitment.

Big companies often know that much of this big-ticket consulting business-school shenanigans is nonsense; but they know they need to be seen to be doing it by shareholders and stakeholders. That's how it all works.

Medium-sized companies – say from £1m to £50 million turnover – don't have the need, luxury, patience or profits to justify that approach. Neither the guru/coach nor big management consultancy approach works for them.

SO what's in the middle ... for the middle?

What will work for the medium-sized business? Well, something that does not have the dictatorial basis of either gurus or management consultancies.

Something that is more collaborative and participative. Something that is more respectful of the client's own experience, expertise and achievements – and more enduring. Something that is a two-way process: each party has something to give – and something to take.

Our peer-to-peer era

We live and work in a peer-to-peer era where knowledge and facts are ubiquitous; and often free, or low-cost. We also live in an era where 'wisdom', knowing the right answer, or the right thing to do, is as rare and valuable as ever; indeed, more so in a complex world with many choices and many wrong paths to go down. Most of us no longer believe (if we ever did) that one person – one guru – has all the right answers.

Most don't believe that 'wisdom' is equally and identically applicable to all situations, all companies, all markets, all of the time. Most believe in bespoke solutions requiring specific, not just generalised, 'wisdom'.

FACT: Middle-market clients want more than just more sales/profits/customers

Most business plans, and all business how-to providers, tend to be quantitatively focused: they talk numbers, KPIs, money, money, money. And of course they are right to start there – no money, no business. Where they are wrong is *stopping* there – failing to take a business on to bigger, better things.

It could be argued that the trouble with these entrepreneurial gurus is that they lack real ambition for the businesses they work with. Many owner-directors not only want to achieve more profits – they *can* achieve more than that, *much* more.

What they want, what they lack, is a bigger picture. This is not about even more profit or even more staff (although it might be); it is more about what it is that directors are trying to create and achieve with their businesses. This nebulous aspiration is best encapsulated in the Greek word, *eudaimonia*.

In search of corporate *eudaimonia*

Eudaimonia (literally, from the Greek meaning wellness or good spirit) is perhaps best-translated as 'human flourishing', and by implication is all about achieving the best possible balance of financial, physical and moral well-being.

In a phrase, getting the best out of life and work: what we want for ourselves, fellow owner-directors (and most shareholders) and for the company. Consequently, it has wider perspectives than pure maximisation of profit.

It's about creating long-term infrastructure solutions that will help build and maintain company growth, higher margins, and, ultimately, higher profits and exit value, but … *not* building it only on financial performance. Respecting that sustainable corporate success requires a great brand, great products, great people, loyal customers, and an ongoing investment in development.

Owner-managers versus owner-directors

The distinction between those who work in and on the business always resonates, but there is a greater divide linked to this.

In practice, very small businesses (let's say under £1m turnover or under £100,000 net profit) are owned and run by owner-managers, who cannot but work in the business day in, day out.

By contrast, owner-directors largely work on their business, while still working *in* it. Their role is more strategic and wide – and their businesses are usually well-established with a functionally defined staff, and a brand (not just a business). Their businesses have a turnover in excess of £1m and up to £50m, and a £500,000 net profit potential.

What owner-directors believe and want

Experienced owner-directors don't believe in miracles or quick fixes. They don't believe in simple formulae for business success, and they tend not to believe in 'gurus'. They tend to have a justifiably high opinion of themselves mixed with real-world, enforced humility.

They think they have some – but not all – of the answers. They know they have done many things right, and failed with many others. They understandably don't want to be preached to, or have their experience and expertise ignored, or undervalued. They want *heterarchy* (a system of organisation where the elements are unranked) not hierarchy. They want to work in a peer-to-peer manner, with mutual respect. Almost everything about the 'guru' approach is wrong for them – and it irritates them.

Owner-directors don't ...

Owner-directors don't want and don't believe the 'MBA In A Day' proposition. They probably don't believe in MBAs, and certainly don't believe you can learn that much in a day. They see it as marketing nonsense that lacks credibility – and consequently doubt the value of anyone who promotes such a thing.

Owner-directors don't believe that their business can be, or needs to be, transformed. They want improvement, not revolution, and they know that improvement is as much to do with how their business operates as anything related to direction or strategy.

They are highly suspicious of 'consultants', especially those who offer high-level strategy without pragmatic implementation, and equally of those of the short-sharp-shock school of thinking.

They are looking for evolution: performance improvement over time, fitness in changing markets.

What is to be done?

I have simply identified what seem to be the real needs of a large number of owner-directors. There is a gap between what the clients want and what the suppliers are delivering. It will be the generation of suppliers who understand the real needs of their clients that will prosper in the future.

However, because of the expert nature of the business support industry ("I am the expert, I know best. Let me help you"), trends have tended to be driven by the supply side, the consultants and not by the clients themselves.

Basically, consultants are giving clients what they, the consultants, think the clients need. 79% of consultants believe they deliver an exceptional customer service. But only 16% of their clients agree. That's a service delivery gap of 63%.

Behind these figures lies the fact that clients want something different from what is being offered and delivered. It is time for the consultancy industry to wake up and smell the coffee!

Ten Top PR Tips
by Peter Ibbetson

Co-founder of JournoLink

You could be forgiven for believing that PR is all about proportional representation, and in a politician's mind, in a marginal constituency, it may well be. Anyone in the public relations industry, though, would of course correct you – PR is all about how effectively a business manages its external profile.

A business without a retained formal PR agency, and which as a result is getting virtually no media coverage, would probably argue that there is no difference. There is an intrinsic link between the level of the PR agency's retention fee and the level of media brand noise created. So, indeed, proportional representation is not far from the mark.

For the sake of this article though, let's define PR simply as brand drum bashing, or dare I say, percussion reverberations. Making a noise in the external marketplace and benefiting from the echo.

So, how does a business, without the big budget to get someone else to do it for them, go about the noise creation for best results?

Here are the ten top tips from Journolink:

1. Don't do it all yourself

Admittedly, this completely goes against the whole concept of having no big budget. The point is that getting your brand message out need not cost a fortune. There are a whole range of alternatives to a formal retained, or even employed, PR resource. At the very affordable end, the likes of Journolink guide businesses through the process of issuing press releases and media content, and then link the businesses to the relevant journalists to optimise coverage. The secret is that it's an online service, without the attendant cost of flash offices and corporate entertainment, meaning that the cost is only a matter of a few pounds every month.

The key is that having the know-how, and access to the right journalist audience, then knowing how to capture their interest, is absolutely fundamental to getting media coverage.

Without that most businesses would be wasting their time trying to coerce third party commentators into writing something good and compelling about them. They shouldn't feel bad about this. Their skill is in running their business. They employ an accountant to make the annual accounts add up; they employ a solicitor to make their contracts hold water. It makes sense to work with even the most affordable PR service to get their messages out effectively.

2. Think laterally

Don't just limit your approach to writing a press release, posting it to the journalist and keeping your fingers crossed that you will find yourself in the headlines.

The media industry is in the middle of a 21st century restructuring. We are rapidly moving on to use social media as much as traditional media. The likes of Twitter have opened up a whole new world of communication, and the obsession with tablets, apps and bloggers is socialising the distribution of business news and content. Commentators are now picking up news as it happens and on the go, and businesses that rely solely on traditional PR placement through 20th century news wires are finding themselves part of yesterday's news.

At the same time, businesses should not think that a 140 character tweet is all they need to post to hit the front page. That's what they need to do to capture the attention, but the journalist will still want the detail, which is why combining traditional means and social means is the real secret to optimising coverage.

The smart agencies, including Journolink, take exactly this approach, meaning that businesses need not necessarily employ their own army of employees doing the lateral thinking. If they aren't doing it themselves, they should certainly make sure their chosen PR partner is doing so.

3. Anticipate your audience

The great temptation is to rattle something out that you understand and which interests you, in the blind belief that the rest of the universe is equally tuned. The skill in getting your news out in preference to any other story is genuinely being the one that is different. The question to ask yourself is, would you pay to buy a newspaper to read the news content that you have put out, or rather would your teenage son or daughter? If not, you are unlikely to entice the journalist to give you column inches.

So spend time reflecting on who you are trying to influence and what is likely to capture their interest. This boils down not just to the content, but also to the way it is presented. Facts and figures; pokes and provocation; quotes and questions all add to the appeal.

Put yourself in the shoes of the reader and assume that the journalist will merely copy and paste your words. If you are happy, then ask the most cynical person you can find. Only if they are captured have you passed the audience anticipation test.

4. The two second hook

You have about two seconds to hook a journalist. Don't assume that you are the only person trying to get coverage. Many journalists simply don't open their emails during their working day because they have so many. The ones that just rely on social media may not be opened at all and may be forwarded straight to the junk box.

Which leaves the headline hook as the most important part of any press release, blog or even short form news release.

Follow the approach the journalists take in their headlines. Be provocative, edgy, compelling, and don't worry too much if the headline has a little 'poetic licence' in it. If it broadly relates to the story, but is positioned as irresistible in terms of reading on, then you have it about right. If the cynical teenager's reaction is "big deal", then the hook is unlikely to land the fish.

5. Tease and tantalise

If the headline hook is effective, you have just won another 20 seconds of the journalist's attention span. This is the time when you have to sell your story. Best described as the executive summary, the first paragraph must tempt the reader to move on to the full story. It must be concise, factual and clinically clear in what you are looking to convey. This is when the journalist will decide if they are going with the story or not.

Focus on providing three sentences and certainly no more than 100 words that are well written and crisp. If all you had was 20 seconds of anyone's time for you to get over what you want to say, it all has to be in this paragraph.

6. Make the body muscle toned

Once you have the journalist sufficiently hooked by the headline and the opening paragraph, you have a pretty good chance that they are now running with your story. So this is where you bulk up with the facts and the content, and deliver the body of your press release. See it as a six pack with each layer of muscle representing something worthwhile. One layer may be some facts from some survey work, it may be some dates, export figures or employment numbers – it's facts that add interest to an article. Another layer will be a comment or viewpoint. Maybe a quote from a local recognised figure, rather than you just saying how great your brand is. You need to use another person's voice to get over why what you are saying is important to the readers.

The body is the part that would enable a school teacher to start a discussion in a classroom. It needs facts, viewpoints and levels of interest that make it worth reading.

7. The little extras

Think about what else you would like to see in an article written from your story. What would add value to it? Frequently journalists will be swayed by case studies. One of your customers willing to showcase how your product really works for them. A situation where it can be seen to be operating in real life. A case where it genuinely has made a difference. Think about what additional colour you can add to the story which would encourage the journalist to give you half a page rather than just a column inch.

Do remember that journalists are often under pressure to fill their space. The more good content you can provide, the more likely it is you will get an increased level of coverage.

8. Don't be shy

A really interested journalist will want to dig deeper into your story and may well look for an interview. So it is important to provide full contact details at the end of any release.

If you work through an agency, they will have the details to give to the journalist, but frequently journalists prefer direct contact. So don't be shy.

You will also find that journalists may look to make contact out of normal working hours, which again emphasises the need to give direct contact details, with availability 24/7.

It's not just the interview that will add value. A good graphic, which may be a logo, a head and shoulders photograph of the quoted person, or a picture of a product in use, is often sufficient to encourage an editor to use your story. Have a look at a newspaper. You will rarely find a page in which there is no photograph. Newspapers and social media channels alike all need graphics, or their coverage would be boring. So, get one step ahead of others vying for the attention of the journalist by providing a link to a good quality, relevant graphic.

9. Timing is everything

This is the clever bit. Don't miss the opportunity to latch on to someone else's moment of fame. This happens all the time in social media, when hash tagging and retweeting gets your brand name out on the back of interest being shown in someone else.

Rather than reacting when you see something of interest, you can also anticipate when a journalist will be looking for a specific theme, and align the timing of your press release to that. At the time of a big sporting event, like a marathon, there will be interest on how to keep fit, what to wear, the best trainers etc. On the announcement of monthly employment numbers, journalists will be looking for case studies where businesses have taken on new employees, or intend to.

Make the most of these diary events. You can research them yourself, or rely on your PR agency to prompt you. If your agency is not doing so, then ditch them. Weekly diaries, like the one that Journolink sends out weekly to all its clients, are key to getting your release out just at the right time to optimise your chance of getting covered. Something that Journolink focuses on too is upcoming awards programmes. Winning an award is almost guaranteed to open the door to some column inches and a photo call.

10. Remember your manners

Once you have a journalist, newspaper, broadcaster or social media audience interested in you, make sure you maintain that interest, Having covered you once, they will be ready to give you another chance. Remember you are helping them fill up their space. You are giving them content, without which they have nothing.

So stay in touch. Even put a phone call in to see what other content they would be interested in.

It's not just the journalists that are your best friends. You can be theirs too if you can provide good content.

The Psychology of Business Success
by Michael Jacobsen

Serial entrepreneur, author and executive chairman of the Global Entrepreneurs Agency

Vision, passion and creativity are the greatest commodities money *can't* buy.

Let's examine vision and passion first. These factors interplay inextricably with an entrepreneur's psychology and completely lay the foundation for any business growth.

Many commentators will say balance sheets, financials and complex business models are the only things that matter and the rest is too *up-in-the-clouds*, but nothing could be further from the reality.

What would Steve Jobs have been without the vision and passion to have changed the world in such a spectacular and far-reaching way with Apple? Possibly an obscure technology academic at a university!

Would Nelson Mandela bereft of passion and vision have been able to stay the course in jail for 27 years and then, in just one term as president, transform a polarised nation of 50 million people into a democracy?

Would Mark Zuckerberg, without vision and drive, be a billionaire game-changer touching the lives of such a large percentage of the world's population, or would he be only a college boy with an interesting and distracting hobby?

Had these leaders not had vision and passion, they would not have achieved what they have, changing the world as they go. This is not just true of high profile, high net-wealth individuals, but of tens of thousands of small businesses around Britain.

Have a vision

What is vision? It is ability to look at what everyone else is looking at, but to see the potential waiting there to be unlocked. It is the gift of being able to dream with your eyes wide open and your energy and intellect fully on the job. It is the ability to see the goal before the journey has even begun. The vision is the setting of the course for the journey.

Vision is standing for something in such a way that others will see what they can achieve if they join you on the journey. It's the light that illuminates the organisation you are building and it's the rally-cry for all those whom you are asking to help you build it. It is to the business what an architect's diagram is to the building of a house.

At school we are taught not to daydream, but in business the leader must daydream. This is the critical time at which the vision will be established and the path to implement it will become clear. Only those who look into the distance can free themselves from the confines of present limits.

SMEs and entrepreneurs should daydream often – in fact daily. Bill Gates was renowned when CEO of Microsoft for taking weeks out each year just to dream and set strategy. Modern companies such as Google are even building their offices in a daydream-friendly manner to encourage all employees to be able to access this part of their brains at any time during the day. They recognise the fact that by encouraging all team-members to access this part of their psyche and feed the results back to their manager, the company gains a combined visionary power supporting the leader. The very windows in your office are an invitation to look beyond its confines. The sky is not the limit; dreams will take you further.

Each year as a mentor, speaker, author and the owner of several SME advisory ventures, I have hundreds of businesses cross my path. The number-one thing that is missing is the permission to let themselves envision. They are usually caught up chasing money, trying to pay bills, dealing with customers, and other day-to-day activities. They feel guilty about taking time off to dream their vision and work on strategy, and in the case of small SMEs they simply have no choice but to be on hand or else the business will collapse. My advice to them is always to make the time, even if it is only a small amount of time per day. Working on your vision and regularly checking in with it is one of the keys to business success.

Talk about the passion

How does passion fit into this?

Passion is the juice that gets you up in the morning, gets you pumped about work and gets you to your desk, even when the tasks waiting for you include paying bills, reviewing accounts spreadsheets and dealing with never-ending emails. Being in a state of passion for your business is just as important in good times as in bad. It is the key emotion that will get you through the *administrivia* more time-effectively and keep your mind focused on the vision.

Being passionate is not just a psychological state: by releasing certain hormones it charges us up physiologically too, thus enabling us to get the tedious tasks out of the way more quickly. Passion in the entrepreneur means dynamism in the business. Many people in business live in a fearful state, but as Dr Bruce Lipton outlines in his book *The Biology of Belief*, this does nothing but damage their health and literally make them dumber by closing off certain key pathways of the brain. Passion is the antidote to this disease.

If you can't get your passion for your business going, it's usually time to exit – to sell it. Look at some of the biggest business sales in the world and read stories about why they sold; usually you will hear them saying things to this effect, even if it's in business-speak such as: "I sold because I had done all I could do with the business," or "It just wasn't exciting me anymore," or more bluntly, "I became bored with it."

So how can we turn these insights to our advantage as entrepreneurs?

Importance of psychology

Successful athletes understand about psychology in sport and consult sports psychologists. They focus, they dream their success and they execute. They do not afford themselves the luxury of prolonged wallowing in doubt before they literally force themselves physically to overcome the misery of past losses, of 4am training sessions, or of not making a particular tournament.

Take Tiger Woods as an example: several years ago he had well documented personal problems which resulted in his once championship ranking suddenly plummeting and staying at this lower level for a few years. Did Tiger Woods, the best golfer in generations, suddenly lose his skill overnight? Was his skill taken from him? Of course not. His personal problems permeated his mindset, and he therefore lost focus and passion for the game. This in turn resulted in rank slipping. The time when he decided that this had gone on for too long was clear: just as suddenly as he had plummeted he rose again; his hunger for success had returned. When asked about this, he replied:

> "I don't want to become as good as I once was. No, I don't. I want to become better."

Vision, passion and psychology are inextricably linked with success in business.

Get creative

There is one other key ingredient in business which is imperative to the long term – creativity. By this I do not mean the kind of creativity we see in artistic creators, such as those practising music, painting and design. What I mean is true psychological creativity, which allows the entrepreneur's mind to solve problems and grow the business from a unique vision. All entrepreneurs are creative – they create or build something where nothing existed before – but the sources of this creativity are passion and vision.

John Kay, the British author of *Obliquity*, says: "If you want to go in one direction, the best route may involve going in the other." Paradoxical as it sounds, goals can sometimes be achieved when pursued indirectly. The most profitable companies are not necessarily the most profit-oriented, and the happiest people are not necessarily those who make happiness their main aim. So this means making time to innovate your business, not just sitting tearing your hair out worrying about how you can make more money to meet this month's bills or this month's payroll. No. Own your vision, live your passion, follow your creative impulse, and these will bring your business to life.

Don't get me wrong. I'm not saying that a business should not try to make money. What I'm saying is that, if that's what you think about all the time, you may not get it. Too narrow a focus can shrink your vision, and too great a preoccupation with day-to-day realities leaves little room for dreams. Go the other way: have fun, focus on your vision and run your business well – this is the way to innovation, which in turn equals success.

Yahoo's Marissa Mayer is on the record as telling Bloomberg News that her greatest challenge day-to-day as a leader is "balancing innovation and execution." It is true in business that you cannot have one without the other. What I am suggesting is that a focus on creativity will almost inevitably engender innovation. Innovation works *on* the business (as strategy, vision and growth) and execution works *in* the business (through emails, meetings and implementation).

Know yourself and your business

To conclude, I would encourage entrepreneurs to understand themselves and their own business psychology. Find out as much as you can about yourself. Know or understand yourself and whatever it means for you. Once you know yourself and your business personality, you can try to change what you don't like or whatever does not serve you. Enhance what you do like and accept everything else.

Clearly each of us has a different business personality and that means we all react differently to different circumstances. By knowing this you can manage your rise to business success better. You can do this by choosing to remain in a positive state of mind – one that invokes the inspiration of your vision, thereby creating passion and thus allowing creativity and innovation to emerge and flourish.

The Mayo Institute in the USA undertook a study which shows that positive people live longer. In the study researchers found that the pessimistic group of patients had a 19% increase in the risk of death when comparing their expected life with their actual life. A lot of positivity comes from being passionate about what you do. If you are passionate about what you do, you are more focused and have greater clarity. You literally move yourself into feeling good and having better health. You work in the flow, lose track of time and everything seems simple.

So what of the many negative situations that we deal with each day in SMEs which may damage our business psychology? Tom Rath and Donald Clifton wrote about such negativity in their book *How Full is Your Bucket?* As pioneers of the field of positive psychology, they studied thousands of people around the world and applied to this a bucket and dipper metaphor – people filling up your bucket or dipping into it. They looked at how our daily interactions with people do one or the other – people either fill up your bucket with positive interactions, or empty your bucket with negative interactions. Being aware of this concept is vital to staying positive and to keeping energetic. The interesting thing about vision, passion and creativity is that when we live them in our business life, as too in our personal life, we are filling up our own bucket, even if others around us are trying to empty it out.

The world's greatest leaders in business have three things in common and these three things are embodied in the business formula: **vision, passion and creativity**. To model these characteristics is to model success.

Keeping Culture, Purpose and Values at the Heart of Your Business

by Jill Miller

Research adviser, CIPD

Your culture, and the extent to which your core values are lived and breathed by your people, has a powerful influence on business success. In fact, this can promote or derail your business growth.

Culture and values will affect the standard and style of customer service delivered, and the satisfaction, engagement and retention of your people, all of which will ultimately affect your organisation's performance. The right culture can also give you an advantage over your competitors, as unlike strategy, culture is hard to imitate. In the words of management guru Peter Drucker, "Culture eats strategy for breakfast."

In his article 'Building Companies to Last', Jim Collins reflects on the timeless fundamentals that enable organisations to endure and thrive. Over six years he studied the founding and growth of exceptional companies that have stood the test of time (for example Hewlett-Packard, Procter & Gamble, Disney, Marriott and Wal-Mart) and compared their stories with those of comparison companies in the same industries which have not done as well. He uncovered how these businesses succeeded from their earliest days by adhering to the same fundamental principles. Collins said:

> "In 17 of the 18 pairs of companies in our research, we found the visionary company was guided more by a core ideology – core

values and a sense of purpose beyond just making money – than the comparison company was. A deeply held core ideology gives a company both a strong sense of identity and a thread of continuity that holds the organisation together in the face of change… Architects of visionary companies don't just trust in good intentions or 'values statements'; they build cult-like cultures around their core ideologies."

In the early days of a business, the culture and how you operate usually just ticks along without much maintenance, and business owners who reflect on this time tend to say, "We all just got it." However, culture is never set in stone and a business's founding purpose and values can easily be undermined or diluted by changes in the business. Left unattended culture and values can develop a life of their own, which can be at a tangent to the principles on which the business was founded. Typically at this point we tend to hear people saying, "It just doesn't feel like it used to."

Business case studies made by CIPD have talked about a tipping point when they needed to focus on actively retaining their culture and integrating key elements of their culture into daily operations. A particular tipping point referred to was when workforce growth meant the owner or leader saw staff face-to-face less on a day-to-day basis. More formal communication methods needed to be introduced as well as devolving responsibility for keeping the message of *how and why we do things around here* alive to other leaders and managers.

Alex Saint, co-founder of Secret Escapes, reflects:

> "I think we've been starting to become aware that at the size that we're at now, it's becoming impossible for us to drive the culture just through the force of our being around. We have new starters every week. So on an individual level, my influence will get less and less strong and we've just been starting to get our heads around how we're going to replicate that founder influence. [We're] trying to work out how we create a process that replicates those values and makes sure that what people would have understood from working really closely with us, they can still understand from a process, rather than getting it through osmosis."

Whatever the signals that the culture is becoming diluted, research by CIPD has found that there are four main areas of the business to focus on to keep what you're all about at the forefront of how you operate. These are discussed in turn below.

1. Formally articulating your purpose and values

In the start-up stages of a business, the vision is usually clear, even if the *how we'll get there* is emergent. It's exciting for everyone in the business as they touch the product or service in some way and are part of conversations around the table about daily progress.

However, as more people join the organisation, team structures are formed and management layers are added, it's necessary to formally embed the business vision and values by writing them down. It can be hard to articulate as it tends to be just something everyone just *got* up till now, but having a common message that everyone can buy into is very powerful. Our case studies have stressed the importance of articulating what the business is about in a genuine way that people recognise.

The key principles for creating a narrative around your purpose and values are to:

- Understand how people talk about what it's like to work here.

- Carefully consider the words you use. Are these the words your people use and do they really mean something to them?

- Recognise where the culture has changed or evolved in a good way.

- Identify where the culture has deviated too far from its founding principles, undermining your service standards or business growth, and needs to be refocused.

- Think about what the culture means for the behaviours and attitudes you expect of people.

2. Helping people to connect with what your business is all about

When you've articulated your values and your vision, it's important to bring them alive for people, helping them to emotionally connect with what the business is all about. CIPD research has shown the importance of having a purpose that people can get really passionate and fired up about; something that's beyond just making profit.

At UKFast, a managed hosting provider, with quite a niche, intangible product (primarily Cloud storage), interestingly it's not the product itself that excites the majority of people, but the means by which the products are developed: innovation. Knowledge of Cloud computing is not essential to work there, but a passion for innovating and leading the market is, since it is central to UKFast's success. Their people need to have a passion for solving clients' problems and coming up with new ways of doing things more effectively. As Jonathan Bowers, managing director, explains, "Our purpose is one that we hint at but we don't have the purpose all over the walls. We will achieve it through innovation and doing things differently as a business. They are the things that drive the team: we do things differently and before other people – going above and beyond for our clients."

Consistent communication across the organisation is essential to ensure everyone is getting the same message, including remote workers. For example, MJF Cleaning devised an intensive training day for staff, which included a section by Martin Ferguson, the managing director, about the company's journey to bring the business's story alive for people. He explains:

> "People don't know where we've come from really, and what I'm going to go into is the risks that I've taken to get the business to where it is now. I want people to know that. I want there to be this sense of urgency, this energy about us again … how we've got to where we are and how we're going to get to where we're going. Then we built on the back of that a bit of a feedback system from staff to help us plan for the future."

MJF also produce quarterly newsletters for staff which reinforce communications from Martin and also profile members of staff who have been noticed for living the company values.

3. Ensure your processes and structure support rather than undermine your desired culture

It's a bit of a balancing act between introducing the structure and process that's needed to guide work and ensure people are treated fairly across the company, and retaining the fundamental purpose and values on which your company was built. For example, some degree of process may be necessary, but too much red tape can curb agility and innovation.

Secret Escapes operates with as little process and red tape as possible. Their aim is to remain lean for a number of reasons, as Alex Saint explains:

> "The ability to get things done, flexibility, speed, the fact that we're in control of our own destiny. Much more importantly than that, I think it's the case that, for as long as possible, people shouldn't be

spending time managing the fabric of the company rather than what the company is trying to achieve. We've been very, very lean in terms of any type of initiatives. I think probably we've pushed back hard so far against too much structure."

What is very clear from CIPD research is that before introducing a new process or structural change to the business, it's vital to think about its potential effect on your culture. How can you design a process so that it reinforces what you're all about?

Similar to most retail environments, Choccywoccydoodah (an art and design-focused chocolatier) need a process by which to measure store performance. The target-setting process has been deliberately set up in a way that reinforces the desired team culture. The most important target to reach is the one for the whole store, rather than for individual teams. Jenna Mullen, London store manager, explains:

"I have a target board and people know what they have to achieve every day. It's broken down into daily for café and daily for shop, and then it's broken down into what we have to achieve for the café for the week and the shop for the week. But, the main figure is the building. Everyone is working hard and that's key. Just because the café has been quiet and they've done cleaning all day, that doesn't matter, they're still working hard. We make the target as a building."

4. Reinforce your culture through your people practices

Your culture and values need to be an integral part of what it's like to work for you. Therefore, every stage of the people management lifecycle needs to be aligned to what you're all about, from recruitment to induction, training, reward, development, and finally departure.

All of our case studies stressed that recruitment for cultural fit was important, with the main message being that many skills can be taught, but attitude can't. Lawrence Jones, CEO and founder of UKFast, explains:

"Trying to find like-minded people is essential. It's not a case of just employing a recruitment agency and hoping for the best. Something we've always looked for from the start, we look for the skills that you can't teach. We look for the people who have taken the same kind of opportunities, who have the paper round gene. It could be a paper round, it could be child-minding, it could be washing cars, it could be doing ironing, whatever people chose to do age 13 in order to take some responsibility, earn a bit of money, stand on their own two feet. Our culture is so defined that the wrong people don't fit in and do more damage than good. We have six core values in UKFast. Every time we recruit outside of these, if we stumble upon a technical genius or someone who appears to have all the skills we require, we get caught out."

It's also important that performance is measured in a way that's consistent with your cultural values, as it sends a clear message to people about what behaviours are accepted and rewarded. Naked Wines have given careful thought to the way they measure performance and how that affects the kinds of behaviours they want to encourage, as the company's founder, Rowan Gormley, explains.

"We don't measure our call centre on calls per person per hour, or cost per call, or length of call, or any of those things. But the measure of the call centre performance, customer service performance, is purely customer feedback in response to the email. When the whole thing [the customer issue] is closed, the person in the Customer Happiness Team closes the case. That automatically generates an email to the customer saying, 'We think we've resolved your issue. Do you agree? Were you happy with it?' Then we look at that score. What it picks up is if we've got somebody who is very quick at getting through calls, and shutting them down, but that actually isn't solving the customer's problem. It picks it up. That's a measure we track all the time, and it's a much better indicator of whether your customer-facing people are doing their job than average length of their call."

In summary

It is clear that culture isn't static; it can be affected by internal and external changes, small and large. Although change has the potential to derail what you're all about, it also presents a tremendous opportunity to reinforce your culture and values.

Although sometimes cultural evolution is necessary and appropriate to achieve the business' aims, straying too far from your founding principles can be detrimental to the business. Cultural dilution can send confusing messages to staff and customers alike about what your business stands for and how it should operate.

For many more case studies on the subject of how organisations have retained their culture, purpose and values over time, do take a look at the full report – 'Keeping culture, purpose and values at the heart of your SME' (**cipd.co.uk/smes**).

From IP to Credible Business

by David Patterson

CEO, Sophia

The key to success is having passion in what you do. I started my own company and I've been fortunate to have worked with a fantastic group of people as we have grown the business.

It wasn't easy, though. The business, Sophia, is an artificial intelligence (AI) based software company working in the online advertising and e-commerce sector. Say *artificial intelligence* to the average man on the street and they will conjure up images not unlike those Steven Spielberg created in his 2001 blockbuster film of that name.

This isn't what we do. We have developed software that uses AI to understand what people are reading online and then intelligently match this to relevant products they will be interested in buying – this enables brands and retailers to reach highly engaged audiences. Sophia's AI technology also improves the consumer's experience online because we don't use tracking technology (such as cookies), and the ads and product recommendations are always relevant and useful to them.

Turning an idea into a reality

Having a great idea

The idea for Sophia came from research I was doing at the University of Ulster, in partnership with Saint Petersburg State University. As we continued to delve deeper into our subject of machine understanding of textual content, I realised the technology we were developing could be used to address numerous critical commercial problems across many different sectors – for example legal, pharmaceutical and publishing. I approached the innovation department at the university and they also saw great potential in our idea, offering us support to spin the company out of the university.

Getting off the ground – being creative on a budget

A major challenge every start-up faces is credibility. The credibility of your idea, your technology, your product and your fledgling team's ability to execute. For building credibility, there is no substitute for paying customers, but it's a chicken and egg situation. One thing we did that really helped in the pre-customer days was to enter business competitions.

For example, we entered and won the 25k Entrepreneur competition, designed to find the next big thing in tech in Northern Ireland, as I thought it would be good exposure for the business. The second competition we entered and won was the All Ireland SeedCorn Award, which included companies from both Northern Ireland and the Republic of Ireland. This competition was judged by national business leaders and investors, and they focused on finding the company with the highest growth potential. The third contest we won – and perhaps the most significant – was the UK-wide Logica Global Innovation Venture Partner programme. This was designed to find a new company with innovative technology that Logica could partner with to accelerate the go to market strategy.

I am not saying this is the only way to build a business, but it worked for us. After winning each competition, the company received more and more interest from customers (who needed less of a leap of faith to work with us), and investors (who wanted to find the next big opportunity). The prize money was useful, but it was the added credibility that really made a difference. It also motivated our team and helped attract experienced people to the company – both employees and board members. In fact, after winning the second competition we secured the largest ever private investment round in Northern Ireland history for Sophia, and attracted Chris Horn (ex-CEO of Iona Technologies) as chairman. This really enabled us to kick start the next step in bringing the company to life.

Location, location, location

History has shown that Northern Ireland is a great place when it comes to innovation and this is where we based our product engineering team. Similarly, Saint Petersburg is a renowned location for technology graduates, with tech giants such as Facebook and SAP based there so they can snap up new talent. Sophia's co-founder and CSO, Vladimir Dobrynin, is located in the city and is heavily involved in recruitment. But for us the big global centre for cutting edge AI technology has to be Silicon Valley, California. So we took the bold move to go west and set up office there. This placed us in the hub of all things tech, accelerated our networking, helped further build credibility and positioned us much more strategically to secure the big US customer wins we were looking for. While this decision brought many positives, it wasn't without its challenges – company communication can be tricky across a 12-hour time difference and it meant a lot more travel for me personally.

One of the challenges at that time was finding the right commercial market for our technology. I used to think it was a great positive for us that it was so generic, but in reality it caused quite a headache trying to work out which of multiple avenues we could pursue. I lost so much sleep thinking about how to find the best market to focus on.

It was no coincidence that a short time after opening our US office we started winning our first US customers. Winning these first few customers helped not only with revenue and credibility, but it also helped us understand where we fitted in the market and enabled us to become more focused commercially. We also wanted to raise an A round of funding to support our growth plans, which we did through Atlantic Bridge (a VC based in Dublin, London and Silicon Valley). Our US customers were pivotal in the process as they inspired confidence for VCs by providing personal perspectives on our product and the problems it solved for them.

Refining our focus

Throughout this time we continually refined our commercial focus based on our experience with customers and what we were seeing in the marketplace. We moved from a model that was more enterprise like to one that was Cloud based. We realised that the best opportunity for us was actually using our technology to understand users' interests online and relating them to products they wanted and we moved into the online advertising space. This was far removed from the plans we initially had for the company, but it was another important lesson learned – the business you initially set out to build may not be the business you end up actually building.

In our case we chose this sector because it had a critical problem we could solve, it was a large and growing sector, and it had a short sales cycle to enable us to get to market as quickly as possible. The markets we had initially thought of as applications, for various reasons, didn't fulfil all these criteria. Once we knew our market focus we set out to add more experience to our board and have recently added Lee Daley (ex-CEO of Saatchi & Saatchi UK) and John Rittenhouse (ex-COO of Wal-Mart USA).

Things I have learned along the way

Making the most of your assets

I mentioned earlier that there is no substitute for the credibility real customers bring. So with each customer win we asked for testimonials. Customers have nothing to lose by telling the truth, so if you have a happy customer with a willingness to speak out, you'll find this makes sales and marketing a lot easier. Often customers know each other and talk. One customer dropping you into a conversation can lead to a quick sale – believe me when I say nothing feels better than being approached by a prospect and hearing "I was talking to a colleague and they said I have to speak to you about your product." Also, happy customers are often willing to help you out, so when you have them, use them to your advantage. If a customer is initially unwilling to help with this, offer them a reduction in fees or a special offer on your product – but get their agreement to allow you to reference them.

Knowing where you need help and seeking it out

Often, one of the hardest things for entrepreneurs to admit is that they can't be an expert at everything and it's not possible to do everything themselves. It is important you can identify critical areas where you have a skill gap and fill it with the best person you can find – areas like sales or engineering, for example. This inevitably leads to handing over some decision-making control (and often equity) to an employee, but it isn't possible to grow your business effectively without doing this. It also helps build confidence with investors, who prefer companies with multi-faceted and experienced teams.

The trickier decisions are around activities you could do yourself, but which are becoming distracting as you grow. Hiring a marketing agency is a good example of this – when I was looking to invest in external marketing, I looked at how much it would cost me in agency fees vs. the value of the time I was spending on marketing myself, which I felt could be used more fruitfully by talking with prospective customers. If you feel your time could be better spent elsewhere and you have the cash, hire a specialist team to run a particular part of the business and hand it over.

Related to this is how to manage critical things like legal advice or accounting. These are key areas for any company, but at an early stage it doesn't make sense to have a legal team in-house. I have always taken the approach of using the best professional services I can find. It may cost more to do this, but I believe it's money well spent and in the long run you will save time, money and heartache.

Be honest – show integrity

Now on to some general principles I try to apply day to day. When hiring new employees, you need to be honest with them. Don't pretend to be further down the commercialisation road than you are to attract who you perceive to be the best salesperson. If they are the right person for the job, they won't need you to promise them the world and they will be excited that you are at an early stage and eager to come on board. If they are not, they will be disillusioned if they do join your company. Also understand that the right person for the job in the early days might not necessarily be the right person a few years down the line as the company matures.

The same goes with investors, don't oversell your proposition. They will find out the truth eventually. If you aren't able to deliver on your business plan then confidence will disappear fast, leading to very uncomfortable board meetings. Be open with investors about the challenges you have, declare them, and instead focus discussions on how you plan to solve them. Every company has problems they need to address and investors will respect you for being honest.

Finally – keep calm and carry on

I was once asked what would be the one piece of advice I wish I was given before embarking on my own business. It sounds obvious, but I wish someone had told me that it's normal in a start-up for things not to always go the way you planned! I used to feel that it was only me that this happened to and that I was doing something wrong. When I realised that this wasn't unusual it removed a lot of stress and allowed me to focus more clearly on alternative solutions. Remember timeframes (especially those involving raising money) are never going to run according to your perfect plan. Always plan for longer than you think for execution.

Steps to Success
by Ami Shpiro

Angel investor and founder of Innovation Warehouse

I n many respects, there has never been a better time for start-ups in London. The capital's dominant global economic and cultural position is encouraging finance, business and talent to move to the city from around the UK, Europe and the world. London is a melting pot of ideas, culture and innovation – and an ideal place to start a business.

The lingering effects of the recession are adding to this: high youth unemployment means there is a huge talent pool for new companies to choose from, while low yields in gilt and bond markets, alongside the volatility of equities, are encouraging financiers to look beyond traditional investments to make a return.

Growth in SMEs has been dramatic – and they now represent 50% of UK GDP and employ 60% of the workforce. Last year, the SME Growth Monitor recorded the highest number of SMEs in the UK since the economic downturn, at 4.8 million.

In the technology sphere specifically, the growth has been even more dramatic, with thousands of companies riding London's tech boom and accessing these ideal conditions for growth – the area around Silicon Roundabout alone now employs 50,000 people. Overall, London is second only to New York as the best location to start a business.

The risks and problems faced by start-ups

None of this guarantees success of course, and the risks for small businesses remain high, with various reports estimating that over half of small businesses fail within their first three years.

In part, this is due to the extreme competitiveness of the market, and this is the natural order of things. A relatively small pot of investment finance for start-ups means that only the best ideas, those most likely to grow, are selected.

But it is also due to a lack of advice and knowledge during crucial early growth stages. The *Financial Times* estimates 20% of failed start-ups would still be running if they had sound advice: this is something that we should aim to remedy.

The government, keen to see more SMEs adding to the economy, has set up a number of initiatives – including Start Up Loans, GrowthAccelerator and StartUp Britain – to offer advice and early-stage funding. While admirable in their goals, these tend to be top-down affairs that do little to assist in the day-to-day running of a small company.

The private sector has more to offer and there has been a huge increase in the number of mentoring schemes. Co-working spaces and accelerator programs in London have helped companies in their early stages. Innovation Warehouse is one of these spaces, using mentorship from serial investors in the tech sphere to advise and guide.

As well as drawing on the experience of mentors, start-ups have much to learn from each other, and we have also set up an environment, or entrepreneurial community, where start-ups in our co-working space can feed off the advice and recommendations of others – not just their seniors, but their peers.

Since start-ups have just as much to learn from each other, who better to offer advice on problems they have faced? At Innovation Warehouse we asked our start-ups what their top pieces of advice would be for other new businesses.

Build your social media profile

"As social media and brand messaging become more prevalent, there is a clear drive towards authenticity. Consumers want to see a company's personality, and if they're not on social media it can be difficult to trust them.

"The era of faceless zombicorps is over. Consumers want beautiful stories behind what they buy, and sites like Facebook and YouTube are the perfect platforms to tell these stories."

– Ed Stockwell, COO and co-founder of Tutorfair, an online marketplace
for finding tutors

Be intelligent about your funding

"Fintech is going through a revolution, and in many respects it is far easier to raise finance than ever before. The angel, venture capitalist and crowdfunding opportunities all mean there's a lot of money floating around.

"However, each method comes with benefits and downsides, so be very strategic in your funding profile over the entire lifetime of your project, ensuring it aligns with your company's growth."

– Leslie Onyesoh, CEO and founder of Kwanji, an online marketplace for making and managing international trade payments for SMEs

Take time to research your market

"Whether you're creating a product or service from scratch or joining an existing company, market research is an invaluable investment.

"Take your time to research your market segment, the competition, people currently working for the company and previous, third party partnerships (if they exist), blogs, and recommendations. Fail to Prepare, Prepare to Fail."

– Jonathan Posner, VP of sales at Whichit, the social commerce platform

Get your pricing right and start hiring early

"B2B pricing is hard to get right and yet critically important. It's natural for entrepreneurs to firstly underprice and secondly not price in the value they provide. There is a growing body of content online to help structure your pricing more scientifically. We made an early mistake in our pricing; fixing it drastically altered the course of the company.

"It is also important to start the process of financing and hiring early. You should start the process at least three to six months in advance. Hiring does not happen overnight and is hard for all growing companies – have a strategy in place and start the process early."

– Chris Padfield, CEO of Deskpro, a multi-channel helpdesk platform

Make sure your business is your passion

"Make your business easy, lucrative and fun. You will have 10 hours in a day when you do what you are passionate about. But make sure you offer real value to your customers, because without them your business is just a hobby."

– Colin Grant, head of marketing and PR at Gamar, a creator of location-based interactive and educational games

Get your culture right and keep responsibilities clear

"As you build your company you're going to be asking your first few employees to work long hours and fail a lot. That's not an easy thing for someone to do if they don't buy into your business. Make sure everyone believes in the long-term vision of the company; maybe even let them shape some of it. Without everyone sharing a belief and passion, it's going to be difficult for people to stay motivated.

"However, in order to build and maintain a good working culture you need to be sure that everyone knows their role. It's never going to be possible to segment roles completely, especially at the early stages of a start up, but time is of the essence and you can't be wasting it by muddling, or doubling up roles. Focus on clarifying roles, or if not roles, then responsibilities, or if that won't work, separate by project."

– Michael Bridgeman, head of business development, Fleximize, a provider of short-term loans to SMEs

Don't go it alone, get a mentor

"Instead of spending days online researching every topic, go to professionals, people who work in the field. Find somebody to mentor you through the process. The chances are they will be able to give you the same or better advice in ten minutes instead of what you would've come up with researching online for days.

"There are lots of people who can help – university lecturers, salesmen, accountants, societies, even business owners – and you can always find an advisor who will *love* to help you, often much more than you expected."

– Justas Cernas, co-founder of Customuse, developing customisable guitars via 3D printing

Find the right structure for your business

"Words and ideas can change the world."
– Dead Poets Society (**Dir: Peter Weir, USA, 1989**)

"The above quote is perfect wisdom from the late, great Robin Williams' character of John Keating. We believe in encouraging, developing and fostering ideas at all levels of what we do and have implemented a flat hierarchy so that everyone believes their ideas can make a difference.

This allows us all to listen, observe, be curious, ask questions, problem solve and make connections."

– Weerada Sucharitkul, director of FilmDoo, an international movie platform for watching, sharing, following and tracking foreign and independent cinema

Don't be afraid to go the extra mile

"It's important to try and contribute more value than is specifically required in immediate commercial agreements. This will help maintain long-term relationships and secure future opportunities. Without your customers your business is just a hobby, so go the extra mile to help cement your consumer base."

– Fiona Triall is COO of Xelsion, the digital media training and consultancy firm

Don't hide your idea, share it

"When entrepreneurs first join our programme they are very protective of their ideas, worrying that someone is going to steal their idea and they'll lose their business. This is because people often associate having a great idea with being a great entrepreneur.

"We strongly believe that it is not the idea which defines an entrepreneur, but the execution. Anyone can have a great idea, but not everyone can turn it into a business. Therefore, we encourage our young entrepreneurs to be open and to talk to as many people as possible.

"By talking to people you can refine your idea, people will give you feedback and they might have helpful people you can talk to. If someone's tried it already and failed, you can learn a lot from them. Of course, there'll always be competition out there (eventually, if not already). It's only when there's no competition that alarm bells should start ringing because it could mean there's no market."

– Zara Pearson is COO of New Entrepreneurs Foundation, an educational charity supporting young entrepreneurs

10% idea, 90% graft

Across all of the start-ups we asked to take part in this article, one overriding point was clear: developing an idea, concept or new product was only half the battle, and in many ways the easiest part. Building up the rest of your business – the BD, marketing, pricing and staff – was far more time consuming and harder, yet essential to the growth of a business.

In my own personal experience, building a successful start-up is 10% idea, 90% graft, and this is where too many exciting, innovative and frankly fantastic ideas fail.

As more competition emerges in the coming years, both at home and from abroad, start-ups need to increasingly think about their business model, especially if they want to get the finance they need to grow.

My own piece of advice, which I have saved until last, follows on from this.

Love is blind

"Be careful of falling in love with your idea, because, as the old adage says, 'love is blind', and while investors will look for your passion, they will also check for many other strongly supportive reasons to invest – and the absolute absence of any fundamental reasons not to.

"Your market research should be dispassionate, and include rigorous attempts to invalidate each and every one of your assumptions in regards to market, your route to market, competition, the barriers to entry, future growth, etc.

"Detached research and preparation is essential in ensuring you are not spending months building an idea that your own passion has blinded you towards – and that is not a viable business."

– Ami Shpiro, founder of Innovation Warehouse

Why Social Media is Good for Business

by Nick James

Founder of Fresh Business Thinking

A nascent novelty at the turn of the new millennium, social media has gone on to revolutionise how we do business. It has allowed companies to personalise their dialogue with customers and send their brand message further than ever before.

For today's customer, the webpage is often the first point of contact – the shop window to peer through to examine what a business has to offer. And for businesses, integrating with digital platforms gives us the opportunity to reach out to customers in so many different ways.

The online world is dynamic; serious time and effort are needed to nurture an online presence that can keep pace with the rapidly changing tastes of the online consumer. While not an end unto itself, social media should be integrated with all other marketing and PR initiatives.

Let's look at what social media can sbring to your business.

Increase exposure customer loyalty

The Internet Advertising Bureau UK released data in July 2013 showing that nearly 80% of consumers said they would be more inclined to buy more often in the future because of a brand's presence on social media. Furthermore, 83% of consumers said they would trial products because of the brand's presence, illustrating the far-reaching potential of online campaigns.

Shareability

Shareability is the magic ingredient: a tweet links to a Facebook page, YouTube or Instagram account and in a few moments your message has been amplified around the globe. Make sure all content you put out bears those small social media icons, these are the launch pads that will get your messages to the people you are trying to attract.

Boost your search engine profile

Search engines now take social media into account when indexing content, which means your presence on the popular platforms will directly impact how your company ranks in internet searches.

Links forged across the social media spectrum are analysed by search engines to rate the quality of your site. The more links your website achieves, the quicker search engines index the content in their rankings. Social media can influence the number of links web content receives in a shorter period of time, and this can often speed up the indexation process of the content in search engines.

Making efforts to connect with your target audience will also help raise your profile. Try to gain followers who are genuinely interested in your business. Attention from reputable sources, as opposed to spam, will raise your credibility with search engines.

Search engines also love fresh and relevant content, so keeping social media outlets alive with quality regular updates represents another chance to attract more followers, more attention and a higher internet profile. When it comes to pushing relevant traffic to your website, the benefits of search engine optimisation (SEO) may take a while to kick in, but the effects will eventually translate into sales.

Generating and warming up leads

Many business-to-business marketers attribute too much importance to brand awareness, overlooking social media's lucrative potential as a lead generation tool. Beyond *likes* and *shares*, user-friendly online forms can be used to grant visitors access to valuable content on your website.

Twitter cards help you drive lead generations, giving users a no-fuss pathway into your business; those interested can share their email addresses with you at the click of a button and without having to leave the Twitter domain. The address book of outdoor clothing company Rock/Creek expanded considerably by over 1,700 new subscribers in less than one week after they used a Twitter lead generation card.

Competitions are another great way of raising your profile and your number of quality leads. Pay attention to what kind of information you require – if you are asking for an email address, make sure you have the customer's permission to contact them. Depending on your business, you will want to know different things.

Remember, the fewer questions you ask, the better, so what you ask needs to be well thought through to give you the results you want, and in a way that does not put the customer off. And think about the reward – if you're trying to attract cycling enthusiasts, don't offer a bread-maker as a top prize.

Costs

The best part of the new world of networking is its low-cost – even no-cost – appeal. This is amazing when you consider what *going viral* could do for your brand's image.

Being so much less expensive than traditional print or mass-media marketing and reaching such huge audiences (e.g. Facebook now has more than 400 million users, and half of these log in to their account every day), online networks are a natural extension to online marketing.

Conclusion

There's so much to get excited about with the potential of social media. By all means get carried away, but in the right direction. Customers who are constantly bombarded with information will not stay customers for too long. Keep your brand visible using images, videos, observations and tips which followers will warm to. The success of Instagram and Pinterest stand as testament to the power of the image over words. Reach for your customers' personalities before their pockets by building social dialogues which demonstrate your company is concerned with more than dry self-promotion.

Social media has opened a whole new dimension to marketing and it's essential that we as business leaders wake up to the creativity and flexibility that customers now expect. Stay true to your core objectives and brand values when setting out your digital stall and embrace the opportunities social media brings to your business.

Crowdfunding

by Henry Catchpole

CEO of Inform Direct

Crowdfunding is a great way for small businesses to raise capital. The beauty is that having lots of people investing relatively modest sums means that businesses are able to raise meaningful amounts. Until recently, financing a business using traditional funding resources – banks, insurance, stock markets and charitable donations – required defined investors to provide large sums. Besides which, it was expensive and time-consuming. But crowdfunding uses the internet as a resource to attract thousands – if not millions – of people to take part in a venture.

Inform Direct was set up initially with the resources available from the founders. But it wasn't long before we realised there was a real market for our product and that it could be developed faster by getting a lot more people on board.

To reach all those potential customers we looked at crowdfunding opportunities.

What it means

In the past, investing in small businesses was the domain of the very rich. But crowdfunding means anyone can experience the excitement (and hopefully reward) of investing in early stage companies. Indeed some crowdfunding platforms accept investments of just £10!

Crowdfunding allows more and more people to invest in businesses that they believe in or have some sort of connection to, without having to risk big sums.

While this is an exciting prospect for many – and gives small businesses access to funding opportunities like never before – it can also be a confusing arena for many because it is presented in such a wide spectrum of ways.

Investments are usually made through online platforms, which then coordinate and administer the fundraising. But choosing the right site requires research.

Where did it all begin?

The first example of a crowdfunded project is thought to have occurred in 1997. Rock band Marillion were unable to afford to tour after the release of their seventh album so American fans used the then-fledgling internet to raise $60,000 so they could play in the US.

Since then the idea of crowdfunding has snowballed and the first official business-related crowdfunding website appeared in 2001. By 2012, there were over 500 crowdfunding platforms online, and February of that year saw the first crowdfunded project raise over £1,000,000.

How could it work for you?

If you decide that the time is right to go down the crowdfunding route, it's important to the success of your venture that you pick the right site. No two platforms are the same. Your choice is going to be influenced by the amount you are looking to raise and the type of investor you are seeking. Consideration should also be given to the stage your business is at. Some platforms suit mature businesses much more than others. Conversely, some platforms are much more geared to start-ups that have not yet established a minimum viable proposition.

What we did

Our quest for online investment meant a great deal of research.

But finally we decided to use Cambridge-based Syndicate Room, which had recently raised funds for a number of other technology businesses. It gave us confidence it had a number of investors ready to back businesses like ours but the final decision to use it was probably swayed by the fact that it was local – despite the fact that after the initial meeting all subsequence correspondence was carried out by email.

Let's talk about money

Nothing in life is free. So once we had identified some suitable platforms we talked about what fees were involved to get the ball rolling. Crowdfunding sites generally do not require much upfront to get your pitch live, and the bulk of the fees are only payable if you raise your minimum amount, which is, of course, a very appealing feature if you have been bootstrapping.

If you plan on encouraging a significant number of your contacts to invest in your business, you should make sure any 'tame' money does not incur the same charges as third-party money.

If you are seeking to raise a substantial amount, you may prefer a site with a high average investment per investor. There is a cost to having a lot of shareholders with small stakes. Be alive to the number of shareholders you could end up with in order to raise the amount you require.

How should you pitch your proposal to investors?

Crowdfunding sites will ask you to pitch your business to potential investors.

I believe the key to a good pitch is being able to explain clearly and succinctly what your business does and what need it meets – the so-called 'elevator pitch'. Only when a potential investor understands this will they have a hook on which to hang the rest of the information – likely market size, pricing, route to profitability, exit etc. Spending time on getting this right will repay itself many times over. Indeed, I am sure that it played a large part in the speed with which we raised funds at Inform Direct.

When preparing your pitch, avoid all temptation to paint a picture that is unrealistic. Your investors are likely to have a good head for business and as soon as they sense a proposition lacks integrity it will be dismissed. So, always be honest, and if potential investors raise a question take the time to give it a full and respectful answer; it will be read by a lot of other potential investors.

What are you offering in return?

Working out what you are offering in return for investment is a very important part of the process and an area where I would recommend that you seek external advice. If the valuation post-money is eye-watering, you are unlikely to attract investors. Likewise, if too little equity is being released this may deter some investors. Indeed, selling a small percentage of the business for a hefty premium can give rise to a misleading valuation that could prove problematic if future funding is necessary. This is because the early investors may resent the lower valuation necessary to secure the next round of funding.

Does it work?

Yes. Inform Direct broke the record for the quickest close on crowdfunding website Syndicate Room. We set out to raise £300,000 on the platform, and managed to attract notable angels, high-net-worth individuals and sophisticated investors who together helped us achieve a remarkable total of £450,000 in less than two weeks.

If you ask me, crowdfunding is a fantastic way to raise funds if the model works for your business. It's a process I'd recommend as long as you're realistic and do the necessary groundwork.

The faith that our investors showed in backing our business has already paid off. In just a year we have had over 3,000 companies register for the service and we expect our user numbers to be pushing 10,000 by 2015. We have a full plan for continually developing the site and the service we offer and as we develop more features we expect the rate of growth to further accelerate.

Leading Your Small Business Effectively
by Ksenia Zheltoukhova

Research adviser, CIPD

The value of effective leadership cannot be underestimated. It can improve employee motivation and commitment, bolster an organisation's potential for innovation and enhance its performance. A lack of good management and leadership, on the other hand, can be an obstacle to business growth. CIPD's recent research shows that there is a real appetite among SME leaders to achieve growth by developing the leadership skills of their managers, but many simply don't have time for formal training or are confused by the wealth of advice available.

In order to understand what leadership looks like in SMEs and to provide business leaders with practical tips and advice, CIPD has looked at the various stages of SME growth. What we have found is that, depending on the maturity of organisational structures and processes, as well as the level of skills within an organisation, the nature of leadership has to evolve for a business to stay successful.

Where does leadership 'fit' in an SME?

Leadership can be broadly defined as the ability to influence people through personal attributes and/or behaviours, to achieve a common goal. It is different from management, which is about planning, organisation, co-ordination and implementation of strategies, tactics and policies. Leadership improves business performance through interaction with people, although different leadership styles can be effective depending on the individual leader and the situation.

Traditionally leadership theory has focused on the attributes of senior executives, highlighting their role in providing clarity of direction for the rest of the organisation and inspiring people to perform. However, recent economic challenges, increased global competition, and customer demands mean that businesses today need to adapt and respond to change more quickly than ever before. This means it's no longer feasible to concentrate decision-making at the very top, and a growing number of organisations recognise that empowering front-line employees to do the right thing on behalf of the organisation makes business sense. As one SME leader we spoke to put it:

> "The world is changing far too quickly for the old style of management. If the exponential rate and pace of change continue, we will see more change in one week in the year 2025 than we did in the whole of the last century. The directors can't possibly believe they are going to keep up with that amount of change, but if you have 120 people trying to keep up with it, you stand a chance, don't you?"

Leading an SME through its growth stages

While there are often different types of leaders in an SME, the role of the business leader or head of the business is to recognise the type of leadership the organisation needs at any moment in time. Unfortunately there is no single 'recipe' for effective leadership, particularly as the rate of change in a growing business will require the SME leader to adapt and re-allocate responsibilities quickly. For example, while inexperienced teams may require a hands-on leadership style, as employees gain confidence business leaders need to take a strategic back seat, leaving the day-to-day decisions to operational managers and front-line staff.

Start-up/entrepreneurial stage

The start-up stage of a business is often characterised by informal and fluid structures and strategies, where everyone has flexible roles and shares information and communicates freely. With only a few 'employees' the business leaders or the entrepreneurs have multiple roles to play, as they balance the day-to-day with the strategic needs of the business. They are often involved in virtually anything that is going on with the organisation, and become at times overwhelmed by short-term 'survival' tasks.

Nick Russell, CEO of We Are Pop Up – a company that connects landlords and tenants of short-term business lets – says that his role involves managing the whole spectrum of internal and external relationships of the business:

> "When you look from a stakeholder view, you have the customers, the founders, and then you have the staff, and then the investors. Even within the investor category, you have family; you have angels, the institutions. Everybody has to be dealt with differently. It's like being a traffic officer at a complex roundabout."

The entrepreneurial edge of We Are Pop Up, specifically its small size and the breadth of experience of individual team members, means that there is no formal hierarchy of managers and staff. Graeme Maciver, software engineer, the only employee with a designated manager, explains there is no need for one-to-ones or project meetings to assign actions, as "[his] day-to-day work is decided on the sprint planning [weekly priority-setting meetings]. It's like peer management of your workload. We organise who's going to be working on what for the next week, and everything that needs to be done is put into a spreadsheet. Then, I just go through it. Having a boss hasn't really impacted me yet; I haven't really had to have a boss yet."

Emerging hierarchy

At the start-up stages of an SME, much of the leadership happens informally through 'peer management'. However, as the organisation grows and new – less-experienced – employees join the business, one of the roles of the business leader is to provide a strong sense of direction, as well as making sure that they are providing their employees with the right role models and coaching to do well in their business.

John Minion, CEO of Yorkshire Wildlife Park, started in the industry as a seasonal animal-keeper when he was 18. While he has vast experience in zoo-keeping, John sometimes finds it challenging to put on a business-like persona when all he wants to do is follow his passion. However, running a business means he needs to constantly review the structures in his organisation and people management processes to catch up with growing customer demand. He says, "[It is] very easy to revert back to [animal-keeping] when things get stressful, because that's what I'm really comfortable doing, I know it inside out. The commercial aspects of running the business I find a real challenge."

John reiterates that balancing the bottom line requires a much more direct approach as the business finds its feet. John says people management is his biggest challenge, as he has to follow a process rather than dealing with staff informally. As the distance between leader and followers grows, it is increasingly difficult for the leader to maintain consistent management practices without treating individual employees like a number.

It is crucial to start nurturing the next generation of leaders at this stage of an SME's growth. If an SME grows rapidly, individuals are often promoted on an ad-hoc basis to plug a gap in service. While the size of the organisation and the complexity of operations may not yet justify a full hierarchical structure, it is essential to plan ahead for the next stage, when specialised functional departments will require skilled middle managers to bridge the growing distance between the senior leaders and the employees, and to communicate the values and the passion throughout the business.

Clare Pearson, HR Manager at the Yorkshire Wildlife Park, says, "Because the organisation developed so rapidly, we've put people in managerial and leadership positions very quickly. We did not have time to give them enough training to get them to meet that level. One of my priorities at the moment is to give them the skills to be able to fulfil those positions in the short window when they're not too busy [with work] to do the training."

Formalisation of processes and structures

As an organisation grows in size, functions diversify and become more specific. At this stage the SME leader has to begin to delegate operations to a team of trusted senior managers while shifting their own focus onto strategic priorities and managing the external relationships of the business.

Delegating day-to-day management is a challenge to many business leaders, who may have been with a business from the very beginning. This is the time when some business owners/founders might leave the business completely, or step away from the operations by appointing a new managing director.

Julie Kenny, currently executive chairman, was a founding and then managing director of Pyronix, a leading UK manufacturer of security and intruder alarm equipment. Julie now has "a helicopter view" of the business, having stepped away from the day-to-day management and focusing on the strategic direction for the organisation, as well as sitting on the boards of other companies. She says: "Becoming chairman of my own company was the hardest thing I ever had to do because I am emotionally attached to the company and the staff. The company was my baby and I knew everything about it. But the baby has grown up and I had to learn to allow people to take responsibility. [The new managing director] challenged me several times to make sure I did that because he has not grown this company and is more emotionally detached."

"I've learned to delegate. I've learned to become a critical friend. Actually I've learned to be a better chairman because now I can see more. I've just got this knack to find where things may be going wrong: as I go around the company speaking to staff, I see things and intuitively know 'That's not right.' I just delve a little bit more and find out the issues."

Established organisation

Where functions have been established, and the processes tested at the previous stage of the SME's growth, the front line has to be empowered to lead an organisation, to motivate and maximise the potential of the now-experienced staff. The role of senior leaders at this stage is to create an enabling environment, in which cross-functional teams can make independent decisions, guided by a clearly articulated vision for the company.

At the established organisation stage, the role of senior managers and leaders is far less hands-on management, and can be characterised as creating the 'binding force' for a fairly large number of internal and external stakeholders. First, the role of the leader is to connect their people to the 'bigger purpose' that the business is trying to achieve, acting as guardians of organisational values, and stimulating employees' engagement with the business. Secondly, the leaders are best-placed to create an enabling context for their workforce, removing obstacles preventing front-line staff from doing their jobs.

Millers Oils, an independent blender of oil and fuel additives, has experimented with manager-less teams in its sales and marketing department. This is part of a strategy to improve the future competitiveness of the business, building individual and teams' capability to identify where they can deliver the most value to the business. Miller Oils asked teams to work to a collective rather than individual target, and to decide jointly on how tasks should be distributed, with a business development manager providing the overall direction of travel.

Jamie Ryan, director, thinks that the role of senior leaders in a mature organisation is to give up power and concentrate on creating an enabling environment for the front line to do its job. He says, "We have been asked, 'If we are doing all this, what are the managers here for?' My answer was, 'We are here to create the environment where you guys can do your job, and grow and thrive.' That is what leadership has to become now. It is not telling them what to do. It is making sure they have got the things and the knowledge they need to do their job well."

Adapt for growth

Unfortunately, there is no magic formula for effective leadership in an SME. Our advice to business leaders is therefore to carefully consider what kind of leadership their business needs at each particular stage of its growth. This means adapting current leadership style, growing the skills that will be required at the next step on the company's journey.

SEO Made Easy
by Ann Stanley

MD and founder of Anicca

S EO, done right, can help you sidestep your competitors and see a 40% increase in revenue.

Search engine optimisation – normally abbreviated to SEO – can be seen as a bit of a dark art and experts often make it sound very technical. In this chapter I've cut through the jargon to tell you what it is, why it is so important and how you can do it yourself.

How search engines work

Google and other search engines (such as Bing) are looking to provide web-searchers with the most relevant and useful websites at the top of the results every time they enter a search term.

To this end, search engines use a range of ranking factors (their **search algorithm**), which determines the order of web pages for each search term within the search engine results. These include:

- technical factors – how the search engines can index and display data from your site

- on-site factors – including the content and the way the pages are tagged

- off-site factors – including the authority of the site and how many links it has received from other sites.

If you are the biggest brand or a leading expert in your industry, your site will have both relevant content and be trusted (i.e. have authority), so it is likely that you will appear at the top of the results for searches related to your product or service.

SEO is a technique designed to improve your visibility in search engine rankings. It works by making your site more useful, increasing the amount of relevant content and developing your site's authority or online brand. There are some significant benefits to implementing it.

The benefits of SEO

1. Drive more traffic to your website

93% of web browsing starts with a search engine and the top listing in Google's organic search results receives 33% of all the traffic – even more significant when you consider that on average six billion searches are made every day around the world.

So by improving your visibility in search results you will increase the amount of organic (or natural) traffic to your website: visitors that have landed on your website by following an unpaid link in search results.

2. Increase online ROI

Because organic traffic typically has a higher conversion rate than other traffic sources, you can also expect a higher return on investment. In fact, a recent study revealed that a content marketing strategy (part of SEO) leads to a 2,000% lift in blog traffic and a 40% boost in revenue.

3. Broaden your reach

As your online presence improves, you will be able to explore and target new audiences through the power of social media, content marketing and PR – all of which are important aspects of a successful SEO campaign

You will be able to tap into niche areas, which through other means of marketing might be too costly to explore. This allows you to broaden your reach and allows you to experiment with different marketing streams to find the ones most fruitful for your business. This brings us onto the next benefit of SEO – its measurability.

4. Access to valuable data

There are a number of free tools you can use to track the success of your campaign including Google Analytics and Webmaster Tools. They provide you with important data on website conversions, ROI, goal completions, the number of visitors to your website (this can be segmented into **organic, referral, direct** and **paid** categories to name but a few), the demographic of your visitors, websites that are sending the most referrals – the list goes on.

The exciting bit about having all of this data at your fingertips is that you can track the performance of your campaign; you can see what works and what doesn't. As a result you can make *informed* decisions about your marketing activities.

So, where do you start?

Undertaking an SEO project

When it comes to starting an SEO campaign it's important to get the foundations in place. This means adjusting your current website or creating a new one that is SEO-friendly – in other words, a website that is easy for search engines to crawl, is optimised for the most appropriate key terms and, above all, is user friendly.

Here are some of the most important things to remember in your quest for SEO perfection.

1. Choose your keywords carefully

First, you should identify which keywords you want to optimise your website for. In other words, what search terms are your ideal customers going to be typing in when looking for products or businesses like yours?

Your decision needs to be based on the **search volume** for each particular key phrase, the competition for that phrase, and the most important factor: the *relevancy* of that key phrase.

2. Signpost with title tags and headings

In a bid to provide users with relevant search results, search engines crawl websites to try and understand exactly what they are about. They store this information and, with the help of some very ambiguous algorithms, decide which websites to display in the search results.

So you must make sure that you structure your site in such a way that it tells the search engines as much about itself as possible. Title tags and h1 heading tags act as signals to search engines, telling them the topic of each page. They are vital.

3. Entice visitors using meta descriptions

Meta descriptions are a summary of a particular page and appear in the search results below title tags. This is your perfect opportunity to address your target audience directly, ensuring they visit your website over your competitors.

Leicester SEO agency for search engine optimisation services
www.anicca.co.uk/**seo**-search-engine-optimisation.htm ▾
Anicca Digital is a **Leicester** search engine optimisation SEO **agency** offering a range of effective SEO services that will help achieve maximum ROI.

4. Optimise your images

A great way to strengthen the relevancy of your page is to include different media formats such as images, infographics and PDFs. If you do decide to include any of these formats on your website, be sure to optimise them by including a key phrase in their alt descriptions.

This not only makes your pages SEO-friendly, it also means that those with visual impairments using special software can understand the context of the media on your website, improving their experience.

5. Link internally

Internal linking helps improve search engines' ability to crawl your website *and* the user experience at the same time. Many websites already include internal links in their main menu to help users find exactly what they are looking for, but this can be expanded by including links *within* those pages to other relevant pages on your website. This allows both search engines and visitors to browse through the entirety of your website with ease.

6. Check for duplicate content

Duplicate content comes in many shapes and sizes and, if left, can lead to penalties from Google. Worryingly, you might not even realise that you have a problem as content can be duplicated on external websites too!

Typically, lots of websites have two or even three versions of their home page, e.g.

- this-is-a-fake-domain.co.uk
- www.this-is-a-fake-domain.co.uk
- www.this-is-a-fake-domain.co.uk/index

While *we* might be smart enough to realise that these are three different URLs for the same page, search engines see three separate pages, which, yep, you guessed it, counts as duplicate content.

If your website has lots of duplicate content you could get hit by one of Google's penalties, which means that your website won't appear in search results or will be pushed to the back of the pecking order.

7. Stand out from the crowd with rich snippets

If you've been investigating the exciting possibilities that SEO holds for your business, you may have heard of structured data or rich snippets.

It's no surprise that online competition is increasing by the day, making it more difficult to stand out from the crowd. One extremely effective way to make sure a user clicks on your listing as opposed to a competitor's is to mark up the data on your site to make it appear as a rich snippet.

Typically, most websites will mark up their data with structured data, but there are other forms of micro data out there.

Here's an example of a standard organic search listing:

App Store - **Cut the Rope**
Read reviews, get customer ratings, see screenshots, and learn more about Cut the Rope on the App Store. Download **Cut the Rope** and enjoy it on your iPhone ...
itunes.apple.com/us/app/cut-the-rope/id380293530?mt - Cached

And here is an example of a listing that includes rich snippets:

App Store - **Cut the Rope**
itunes.apple.com/us/app/cut-the-rope/id380293530?
★ ★ ★ ★ ★ 6,791 votes - $0.99
12 Oct 2011 – To buy and download **Cut the Rope** by Chillingo Ltd, get iTunes now. ... We're proud to announce that **Cut the Rope** is the world's first iOS ...

This example includes star ratings, price and an image of the product. It takes up more space in the search results, is more prominent and provides more information to the user.

8. Lead the way: XML sitemap and robots.txt file

If you want to control which pages of your site search engines crawl and don't crawl, and which pages they prioritise when they *do* crawl your website, you should implement an XML sitemap and a robots.txt file.

An XML sitemap, as the name suggests, is a map which allows search engines to crawl each page of your website with ease. However, if you want search engines to prioritise particular pages over others, then it's important to include priority levels.

A robots.txt file allows you to tell the search engines which pages you don't want the search engines to crawl and index. This might be admin pages or pages which contain private customer information.

We've covered just a handful of optimisation techniques and there are lots of other aspects you should consider when trying to make your website SEO-friendly.

Develop a content marketing, social and outreach strategy

Once you have the basics in place, the next step is to focus on building your online authority. There are lots of ways you can achieve this; above all, I recommend that you establish a content marketing strategy. This should work alongside your social media strategy, whereby you reach out to bloggers and key influencers in your industry.

The benefits of content marketing

Content marketing is the key to success. If you want to push your online presence you must create a blog with useful, interesting and valuable content for your target audience to enjoy and share. 50% of consumers' time online is spent engaging with custom content. Not only that, but blogs give websites on average 434% more indexed pages and 97% more indexed links. Plus, 61% of consumers say they feel better about a company that delivers custom content and are more likely to buy from that company.

Content marketing can help you to:

- build brand awareness

- establish your brand as an expert

- build natural link profile for your website

- drive targeted traffic to your website

- build a relationship with your target audience.

To achieve the best results you need to develop a content-marketing strategy with aims, objectives and desired outcomes.

Social media and outreach strategy

You must also increase the visibility of your content by devising a social media and outreach strategy. Content, social media and outreach should all work together.

Great content gives you something valuable to share with those who are interested in what you have to say. It also allows you to reach out to key influencers and bloggers who may have previously been unaware of your brand. By using social media and email to reach out, you are increasing the likelihood of gaining links to your website (which will increase your authority), and social activities on and off your website can increase your brand awareness.

Conclusion

As you can see, there are lots of benefits to running an SEO campaign for your business. However, it's important to remember that online success rarely happens overnight, and that an SEO campaign can take anywhere from six months to a year to produce noticeable results.

Good luck and happy optimising!

Resources

- searchenginejournal.com

- business2community.com

- searchenginewatch.com

- blog.hubspot.com/marketing/13-spooky-stats-to-scare-your-boss-into-better-marketing

- www.inboundwriter.com/content-marketing/infographic-the-anatomy-of-content-marketing-2

- www.customcontentcouncil.com/news/roper-finds-majority-consumers-value-custom-media

A Passion to Help Others
by Karen Betts

MD of Nouveau Beauty Group

It was the love of my family that prompted me to take my first job as a supermarket checkout girl at the age of 15. Pensions were low and my granddad struggled with the rent on his council house so I took the decision to buy it for him. I saved my wages, sold secondhand clothes on a market stall and toured the streets selling homemade soap and baked goods until I had enough money for the deposit for a mortgage. My ability to make the repayments was never questioned and by the time I was 17-years-old I owned my own house where my granddad lived.

I qualified as a hairdresser and had a mobile business visiting my clients in a homemade kit-car by the time I was 18 and by the age of 24 I had grown out of the mobile business and re-mortgaged the house to purchase a building and set up my own salon. The business was quite successful and ticked all the boxes until I encountered the first major obstacle in my career. I had a client who had survived cancer and was left with no hair or eyebrows. The hair was not a problem, as I could supply or make her a wig; but the brows were more of a challenge.

There was this new thing called the internet which was proving to be quite a reliable source of information and there was a treatment which was becoming popular in the States called **permanent make-up** which is a form of tattooing. I had a tattooist working in my shop in a rented room so I asked him to teach me and I would use my artistic flair to do the lady's brows. This was met with some derision as no equipment, inks or techniques were available that would be suitable for creating anything other than a pair of blue slugs on the lady's forehead – a scenario we will hear about later on.

So, with my case packed and my boyfriend kissed, I was on an aeroplane on my way to learn a whole new career in America. Some time later, I returned to provide my client with the perfect set of eyebrows that she had longed for. As I had now joined the world of permanent cosmetics, I learned that I was not the first to bring the craft to the UK. It had already gained something of a reputation. A small group of doubters were convinced that permanent make-up was the devil's work and the only options available were those good-old blue slugs for eyebrows. And indeed, there was only a small number of technicians and most were turning out exactly that kind of work using tattooing inks and equipment.

So I found myself not embarking on a new career starting from zero and trying to build it up, but in an industry somewhere considerably below zero, with a tarnished reputation that would need dragging out of the gutter before I could make a go of it.

I discovered a professional body in the USA that promoted the merits of permanent cosmetics and enforced professional standards for practitioners. I joined, and travelled back and forth to the States to constantly improve my craft, and my career and reputation flourished as a result. My partner resigned from his business as a civil engineer to help promote me and the services I offered and we spotted a huge gap in the market. There were a very small number of places you could train to do permanent cosmetics in the UK and even fewer were doing it to a standard that we felt was acceptable.

With the knowledge I had gained from the States and the high standards that I worked to, the opportunity to pass this on to others was immense. Initially I started the school with another very experienced technician who soon left and set up in competition, but the training course that myself and my partner designed became the industry standard in the UK and abroad and was copied by many. Nouveau Contour Permanent Cosmetics was the most well-respected training academy in the UK and our qualified students were the most well-respected technicians as well. As my reputation was growing I had been asked to appear on a number of reality TV shows such as *10 Years Younger* and *Extreme Makeover* and the industry as a whole was benefitting from the positive publicity permanent cosmetics was receiving.

All seemed to be going swimmingly, until I was met with another massive life-changing challenge. I was able to transform the lives of cancer patients and those with alopecia by providing them with the hair and brows they so desperately needed following hair loss, but what about their eyes? With no lashes, the edges of the eyelids are not quite complete. I could apply permanent eyeliner or an enhancement and I could even feather the look to mimic lashes, but it wasn't the same as an actual eyelash.

I was soon on a plane to Hong Kong to attend the world's biggest beauty show. My main purpose for going was to find a solution for my client's missing eyelashes. I was accompanied by my partner, Dave, and a fellow Nouveau Contour trainer, Bridgette Softley. We spent the whole of the time at the show looking at skin lasers, nail gels and lip-growth serums when, in the corner of a small shell-stand, we spotted a young Asian girl fiddling about with someone's eyelashes. We hung around for a while and learned that it was eyelash extensions. She was applying fake lashes from a bag of what looked like the sweepings from a barber shop and sticking them on with black superglue. The client's eyes were streaming with water and the treatment was taking hours, but the seed was sewn and, armed with a bag of the sweepings and some special glue and very pointy tweezers, we were on the way back to the UK to launch a new business. Bridgette was giddy but Dave was sceptical (Dave is always very grounded and carefully assesses every idea I have, often offering a more realistic view to the one I have) but when I waved the bag in front of his face and said, "These will buy you that Ferrari", he came round to our way of thinking.

Bridgette and I spent many hours playing with the lashes and developing our application method. We started to create a manual by which we would teach the new treatment. Within a few months we were ready to launch.

We weren't the first with the lashes in the UK. By the time we were up and running, a UK distributor had been appointed and we had to buy from them. This wasn't much of a problem initially, but as the newly launched Nouveau Lashes was taking off like wildfire, we outgrew the distributor in a matter of weeks and were placing orders that they could neither fulfil nor finance. Dave was quickly on the case and worked tirelessly to find a manufacturer of the products. Everyone says they can manufacture but very few actually do. Most suppliers will take your money and then go and get them made, doubling the price as they do so. The manufacturer was sourced and the bulk order was placed. Nouveau Lashes was now independent and was not being held up by a middle man and was on the road to success, jointly steered by Dave, Bridgette and myself.

At this point, the company hit a bit of an obstacle. We had Nouveau Contour and Nouveau Lashes, both based in the same premises. We had been forced to move out of the original office above my hair salon some time back as we had six full-time staff and only five chairs. We rented office space on the local high street but that was now becoming difficult as we had stock and orders to think of. As a temporary measure, we moved the whole bang shoot into our own house, converting the living room into an admin office, the dining room into sales and the utility room and a downstairs bedroom into accounts. The garage was turned into despatch and warehoused all the products. As Nouveau Lashes had also become international, the garage was also import and export as well. (Where was Dave going to put his Ferrari?)

Time passed and the house got fuller. The commute was easy but we needed more and more rooms to dedicate to the business and we finally cried "Enough!" when we were reduced to one bedroom for sleeping, one for a living room, a kitchen that doubled up as a staff room and our bathroom. As business space was tight in the area, we decided to move out and leave the business behind. The purchase of the house dragged on and on and when it was looking like falling through, the building next door to the salon came up for sale. It was an old pub that had been shut for some time but re-opened and was in financial difficulties. The brewery wanted to offload it and we needed space. On inspection, the upstairs rooms of what used to be a hotel were ideal as offices and training rooms and with extensive bars, a function room and a cellar, we were in luck.

Around the time of all this upheaval, another Nouveau Contour trainer had presented me with an idea. Nilam Patel thought there might be some mileage in an old Indian tradition of **threading**. It's a traditional method of hair removal which we thought we could make popular in the UK. As threading on its own didn't seem all that exciting, we created a whole new concept based on the seven steps of eyebrow preparation.

With our already-established knowledge of the beauty business we were able to quickly establish a range of products to complement the brand, and the whole concept was immediately embraced by our huge database of happy customers. The concept spread like wildfire.

It's 30 years now since I first set out as a checkout girl, then working for myself as a mobile hairdresser. The salon is still going over 20 years on and some of the original staff are still there. I still work in the salon every week and keep a watchful eye, but I have a manager to run it for me now.

We have owned Nouveau House for seven years. We had 20 full-time staff working for Nouveau Contour and Nouveau Lashes when we moved in back in 2008 after its refurb. It was a financial disaster as we bought the building about 20 minutes before the property slump and a year later it was worth a quarter of the price we paid. We've managed to survive the recession despite this and the beauty industry seems to have weathered the storm pretty well. My companies and my business partners and co-directors seem to be doing well; I judge this not by money in the bank or the car I drive (1998 Porsche Boxster) but by the amount of people who I have to book for the Christmas party. In 2013 we had almost 140 but we will need a bigger venue for 2014 as the company headcount is already over 155.

It is quite a feeling of achievement when you stand up and hit a glass with a spoon and there are 155 smiling faces looking back at you waiting for you to thank them for all their hard work.

How to Win a Pitch
by Sarah Shields

Executive director and general manager, Dell UK

G etting a fledgling business off the ground and on the path towards growth is no mean feat and demands great commitment and energy. But, as any entrepreneur will attest, one skill that continues to play an integral role in a start-up's journey is the ability to pitch successfully. Regardless of whether you're trying to secure investment or convince a new lead to sign on the dotted line, persuading someone to believe in you and your company is fundamental to growing a business, irrespective of its size.

Two entrepreneurs all too aware of the importance of the perfect pitch are David Monks and Jordan Fantaay, the winners of Dell's Startup-in-Residence competition. According to Fantaay, CEO of 'smart' email and messaging software provider, Fantoo, and Monks, founder of mobile business intelligence specialist, iNovar, enthusiasm and passion are at the heart of selling an idea – and were key to their success in the competitive pitch to win technology, mentoring, office space and more from Dell.

But the ability to convince others of your business proposition takes more than enthusiasm and passion. I caught up with Monks and Fantaay to get their advice on how to win an audience – from customers, to investors.

Define your goals

You won't always be pitching à la *Dragons' Den*; sometimes it will be simply a first conversation with a potential partner or business lead. But nobody likes having a meeting for the sake of it. Be sure to define why you're all in the room, what you're looking to get out of the meeting, and why you are pitching to them specifically. Think about what your audience might want and your mutual goals. Think about what your audience can do to help your business idea along and ensure that you have a clear 'ask' as part of your pitch. This should dictate the flow of the conversation.

Know your audience

Any pitch must be tailored to who you're addressing. Speaking of the Dell Startup-In-Residence pitch, Fantaay notes: "The Dell team was different to the usual investor audience, so we were careful to communicate the right message to generate the right discussion." Tailor your pitch to your audience from the outset. While a customer will want to know which of their problems your solution can solve, a potential partner will want to know what you're building and why it matters.

As Fantaay suggests, knowing the person's name, job title and why they're in the room is important, as it will allow you to plan who you can direct each point to. For example, the head of operations isn't necessarily going to be interested in expected sales, but may be interested in how you would integrate your system with theirs. Ask qualifier questions to ensure you're targeting the right person with the right message.

Be interesting

Being concise and compelling is key. Your business proposition may be the most interesting idea you've heard, but it needs to spark the interest of those on the other side of the table too. Avoid repeating the same old presentation for a given audience, as you'll appear scripted and your audience will see that.

As Monks points out: "Be enthusiastic: if you can't get excited about your business, then why should they?" He suggests that entrepreneurs pitching for investment film their rehearsals: "Watching the video back through the 'investor's lens' can help identify mannerisms or speech that could be distracting to your audience. No matter how many times you've given the presentation, a regular review will almost certainly lead to areas you can improve upon."

Show progress

From his experience speaking with potential investors, Monks says a common response to a pitch is: "We'd love to invest, but don't want to go first" – this is, in effect, a sign that you've not 'hooked' them yet. While passion and drive for your idea will take you so far, be prepared to provide rigorous detail showcasing the growth and projections of your product or service. Whether it's a five-year development plan with realistic goals or a client testimonial, having a proof point is vital in showing your audience you mean business.

Why you?

Be mindful that your pitch audience is not just looking at your product or company – they're looking at you! You are the person in front of them in that meeting, the face of your business, and the person trying to convince them to take action. Think about the personal assets you can bring to the table and what makes you different from the competition. Is it your background, the network you're tapped into, or are you simply personable and able to connect effectively with your audience? Whatever it is, just remember to show your audience who you are and why they should take you seriously.

Winning a pitch isn't a simple task – it takes a lot of hard work and dedication. But by thinking before you jump in, planning thoroughly and proving your value to the audience, you can give yourself the best chance of success. Perhaps the most important point to keep in mind is that there's no such thing as 'losing' a pitch. As Fantaay notes, "There's always something to learn from any pitch" – so use each pitching experience to your strength.

The Importance of Niche
by Liz Doogan-Hobbs MBE

*Former water-skiing world champion, founder of Liz
Hobbs Group events company*

As a successful sportswoman I am used to having to work
hard and fight for what I want to achieve. I believe that
in business I have, without realising it at the time, applied
many of the same principles that helped me to become
World Water-Ski Racing Champion.

Overcoming adversity was a lesson I learnt early on, when I had to
recover from a near-fatal water-ski accident. I was determined to
compete again and win back my title – much to the horror of my parents,
who had been with me in the hospital (my dad had also been driving
the boat when I fell). I had lost pretty much all my muscle bulk and had
to work extremely hard to build this up again. Three to four stone of
muscle bulk takes some building, believe me. I had been told I was lucky
to still be here, let alone walk again. Sheer determination at this point
saw me through, together with the support of family and friends who
believed in me. The same people keep me grounded now and give me
honest feedback too!

The link between sport and business becomes clearer when you
understand how I made the transition from one to the other. Following
on from my sporting career, when I retired at just 28, I was faced with

the question "What do I do now that I have achieved my life's ambition?" The answer for me was simple: get a new ambition.

As a sportswoman I followed the motto drilled into me by mum: "First is first, second is nowhere", and this led to me thinking about niche opportunities. A niche, to my mind, is something which does not exist by itself but rather is created by identifying needs or wants of people which are not currently being addressed by someone else and offering the solution. It is usually a specialised activity suited to your interests and abilities.

So, as a sportswoman, what interests and abilities did I have? Well, I had trained in sport and business management and had a keen interest in all sports. In my personal life I also kept horses and had ridden for years. I had also worked with people in the entertainment industry and understood how the business worked. This led to me representing people who worked in the sport and entertainment industries; I didn't know it at the time, but this was the start of my thinking like an entrepreneur.

I was looking after Channel 4 racing commentator, Derek Thompson – Tommo as you may know him – and one day went to Epsom racecourse to talk to the managing director about him. We talked about entertainment in general and I suggested I supply entertainment for the Derby. The MD gave me £5,000 as a budget and I provided the full plan for Derby-day entertainment and my girlfriends helped me manage it.

I accepted the challenge and headed off to start researching. My first stop was at the nearest garage where I offered them £5 for their *Yellow Pages*! I then checked what entertainment had been previously supplied and suggested better. The entertainment was good and it added value to the day – people really enjoyed the music and the change in the feel-good factor was noticeable.

Racecourses had never really utilised entertainment to add value and increase the enjoyment factor and I saw an opening that I believed could really help a sport, bring more enjoyment to the day for racegoers and potentially therefore add revenue to gates, which at the time were dropping significantly. I believed there was an even bigger opportunity to increase the attendance at race meetings by giving people extra value for their ticket price. I looked at why people were going to racing: hardcore racing enthusiasts, people who had been with their parents growing up, even people who had never been before but been taken along by a friend.

A day at the races can be daunting when you have never been before; adding music and entertainment softened the race meetings, making them more accessible for a wider variety of people. It meant they were not intimidated and were more likely to return again. It proved right and a male-dominated environment started to open up to couples and families. We experimented with demographics by providing kids entertainment and seeing how the attendance varied – it did, dramatically.

So Liz Hobbs Group (LHG) started full-blown concerts after race meetings. Our first artist was Gerry and the Pacemakers, a normal crowd of 1,500 became 6,500 – and racing and music was born! Music and sport became my driver. I realised I could empower sporting venues, as well as artists, and change the face of both forever. My initial goal was to add value to the ticket for people who were already coming racing. I realised that I had achieved this goal just by delivering a concert and I needed to take it further.

I faced stiff competition from racing purists who felt that music had no place in racing and they had no qualms about telling me so. But, I persevered and concentrated on showing that by adding music after racing it was not detracting from the racing but rather opening up the racing world to a larger audience to ensure the sustainability of the sport in the UK. People were watching their finances like never before, so adding value was vital. By identifying this I was able to offer the solution – no additional charge for attending a race day but a concert thrown in for free. Later, we increased the level of artists and ticket prices were increased minimally to accommodate the higher artist fees, nonetheless the increase meant you still got a ticket cheaper than at a stadium concert most of the time, but with the added benefit of three hours racing with friends beforehand.

It seems so simple and obvious talking about this today, as the majority of racecourses now offer some form of music and/or entertainment on key race days, but at the time I came up with the concept you would have thought I had suggested the horses going round the track on roller-skates! But this is exactly what made the idea niche in the first place. Full-blown, properly staged music and racing did not exist, but by identifying that people would see the offering as added value and would therefore be more likely to go with a group of friends meant I could offer the solution.

My knowledge and experience gave me ideas that others had dismissed. That revenue stream is now worth £3m net to the Jockey Club annually and underpins so much of UK horse-racing to this day.

People have said to me that it is just a music concert after a sporting event. I would challenge that: it has become so much more. The revenue raised by increased attendance allows the venue to reinvest money back into sport. The concert also delivers a unique customer experience as every concert is different. By working closely with the venues we can determine the type of artist who will be most popular and therefore who they should select. What started off as me identifying a need to book artists morphed into an analysis of how to support the venues with their plans for growth. We work with venues, who all differ in their approach, to ensure they are working towards their business plans, in line with their strategy. Anyone can pick up the phone and make a booking. The skill is in understanding the big picture and working together to achieve the goals set with venues, ticketing agents, marketing partners and artists. It's been proven time and again when other companies have tried to work in our space and we've watched it happening again this year.

To be able to identify the needs and wants of a client can be a challenge as they can change constantly with people moving around between businesses too, so you need to be sure that you are constantly reviewing these needs and are one step ahead ready with solutions to challenges, which sometimes have yet to be identified. Identifying risks is akin to identifying a niche, you need to be able to look past what is there and see what cannot yet be seen.

Risks can come in many forms: financial, physical or emotional. As an entrepreneur you have set up a business in a new area and face numerous possible risks. How many of us have watched an episode of *Dragons' Den* and thought "How on earth did you come up with the idea for that?" The key is to have faith in what you are pitching and stand your ground when you are challenged. I am not suggesting you are stubborn and closed to feedback to help your idea develop. But if you have done your research, tested your theory and made adaptations to ensure it will be successful then you have absolutely earned the right to be confident in your idea.

Identifying the niche idea is half the battle – the second part is how to make a success of your idea. How will you grow your idea? Will it be fast 0–60mph growth or will it need to be nurtured and develop more slowly? Should you involve someone who can add value to your idea to help it to grow more quickly by allowing them to join with you, bringing their interests and abilities with them? As an entrepreneur you have a tendency to move at a much faster pace than others so this is something to consider when thinking about joining with someone else. There is nothing more frustrating, for both parties, than having differing drivers and paces. But equally having someone to share in the excitement and development of an idea is priceless. But maybe that's for another day...?

As with all great ideas, the devil is in the detail. To be successful you must have exacting standards and an eye for detail, or at least work with someone who has! This will allow you to develop your ideas by analysing what works, what doesn't and your interests and abilities will give you the insight that others may be missing – hence you coming up with the idea that everyone else wished they had thought of first.

Finally, be adaptable. As an idea grows, the market around it may well be changing. For your idea to remain a success it will need to be adaptable to change, and you may also need to change to keep pace with the idea. Adapting means continuing to learn. As soon as you think you have nothing left to learn you will stop growing and developing. If a niche idea is one which is linked to your abilities then to continue to develop niche ideas you must continue to develop your abilities.

In summary, to be successful as an entrepreneur you should ensure that you achieve the following:

- stand out as a person in your own right – be memorable

- develop a business that stands out from the crowd

- think of an idea that others will kick themselves for not thinking of

- ensure the idea has quick growth potential in an uncomplicated way

- stand your ground – have faith in yourself and your ideas.

Looking back on setting up LHG I realised that the idea that started it all was niche, but it was how I took this idea forward that opened up new opportunities, not just as a business for me and for the venues, but also for me as a person. I love what I do and no two days are ever alike and that's important in your business life. Remember you are only as good as your last good idea, so keep thinking.

Creating and Maintaining Momentum

by Stephen Fear

The British Library's Entrepreneur in Residence and Ambassador

Within the past year, Britain has fulfilled its entrepreneurial potential as, according to a recent study from national enterprise campaign StartUp Britain, there was a record number of businesses starting up: with over 500,000 companies launching in the UK in 2013. This research was also backed up by government statistics which suggested that 95% of the UK's business landscape was made up of start-ups. With government initiatives and schemes in place to promote entrepreneurship in the UK, it's no surprise we are seeing more start-ups than just a few years ago.

For many entrepreneurs, launching a business can be the most exciting time. Putting so much effort into your ideas and seeing them take form is a great achievement. However, I have spoken to a lot of start-ups in the past that feel as though they have reached the finish line by simply getting their business off the ground. In reality, this is when the hard work actually begins.

After exerting so much energy just to get your business up and running, creating and maintaining momentum after the initial launch can be a difficult and daunting prospect, but it's a necessary step to ensure sustainability and lasting success.

Momentum is the measurement of movement that can help decide how high you will go and how quickly you will get there. In business terms, assessing a company's momentum would be accumulating a series of small, but vital, successes one after the other.

With more businesses launching than ever before, it's important that these new companies are prepared for the hard work that lies ahead. Whilst it can often take a while for a business to establish momentum, by simply following these five steps, you'll find yourself better prepared to create and sustain momentum and you will find your company on the steady path to success.

1. Set your goals

Being prepared is often one of the most important, and sometimes overlooked, steps to gaining sustainable momentum in your business. Following the launch of your company, it can be quite tempting to rush ahead without being properly prepared. This can could lead to a number of pitfalls and setbacks.

Putting together a plan for both your short-term and long-term goals will ensure that you know what is realistic and achievable. It's also important to continue looking back at your plan along the way to see what you have achieved, to measure your company's growth and to continue to drive momentum.

Once you have your plan in place, you need to remain focused on your business's strategy and desired outcomes. No matter what your business's goals are, or how you plan on achieving them, creating momentum to reach them starts with your unwavering commitment to your business.

Of course, it's wise to stick to the plan as closely as possible, but it is also important to understand that there are things out of your control – so planning for unexpected occurrences, whether these be professional or personal, is also advised. Obstacles will arise and dealing with them efficiently will reduce stress and put you back on track.

2. Play to your strengths

When speaking to small business owners, they often ask for advice on how to take their business from one stage to the next. Understanding your individual strengths and using them to your advantage will not only allow you to sustain momentum but will enable you to drastically increase it.

Many business owners fall into the trap of trying to do too many things at once, or trying to do things they lack the skills at doing. Identifying your strengths, and being aware of your weaknesses, allows you to see areas that your business excels in. It also gives you the opportunity to see areas that may need work.

Furthermore, research has shown that the reason we perform best at the things we find easiest is because it reduces stress levels. So not only will playing to your strengths drive momentum, it could also lead to a happier working life.

3. Take control of your spending

Contrary to popular belief, driving business growth isn't about how much money you have but how you spend the money you *do* have. No matter the sum of money available, make sure you plan how to spend every penny and try to take into account any unforeseen expenses and non-fixed overheads.

Whilst overheads will depend on the type of business you run, it's important that you take control of your company's outgoings at an early stage. As your business continues to grow, keeping on top of your expenses can become increasingly difficult.

So get to understand your company's spending habits. Just because there has been an increase in customers and workload doesn't necessarily mean there will be an automatic increase in revenue. As a growing business it can be tempting to think that once you have a stable customer base and steady income you can be more nonchalant about your expenses. However, this is one of the biggest mistakes a business can make.

There are a number of accounting software solutions on the market to help simplify the tracking of your business expenses. Once you have an understanding of which areas you are overspending in, you will be able to identify the areas in which you can trim the fat. Whilst this kind of software is certainly useful to small business owners, keeping control of your finances also relies on your attitude towards spending and how you use your company's money. If you find you are the type of person who likes to splurge on the finer things, it might be time to get someone to help you tighten the purse strings.

4. Focus on the results

At its very foundation, business momentum is based on results achieved rather than efforts made. This doesn't necessarily mean that every idea you have has to be a success – failure is to be expected, particularly at the very early stages of starting up. It does, however, mean that you need to concentrate on ideas that work – those that achieve clear, positive results.

It can be easy for business owners to overlook the smaller, short-term successes because they find themselves too focused on their long-term goals. However, it's important to acknowledge all of your accomplishments.

When identifying your successes it's useful to understand how they were achieved and how it could impact your overall business growth. In addition to this, you should recognise your accomplishments as they happen as a way to directly see your business's continued momentum.

5. Stay positive

"If at first you don't succeed, try and try again", should be the motto for any business owner. It's easy to lose focus and motivation at any sight of a setback or obstacle but it's important to stay positive and celebrate even the smallest of successes.

When starting up it can be easy for scepticism and pessimistic thoughts to occupy your mind. Whether dealing with dissatisfied clients, money worries or slow internet, it's important to let those negative thoughts wash away.

Thinking positively puts you in a mindset that enables you to succeed because instead of seeing challenges in front of you, you see opportunities to be overcome. By viewing negative situations as a positive thing, you are more likely to engage with them, think of a solution and ultimately sustain momentum as you drive your business to success.

The key to having a successful business isn't just about having a great idea; it's about perseverance and belief in that great idea to help the overall growth and make it a sustainable business.

No matter the field you work in, building business momentum is about accumulating a series of successes one after the other. Whether this is an increase in sales, meeting set targets or even generating steady business growth, the momentum you achieve will influence the future and longevity of your company.

Once momentum has been established, you'll begin to notice that your determination is paying off and not only are you working hard, but you're realising your goals and continuing to drive your business forward. As you begin to feel the sense of achievement that comes with this, it will continue to encourage you further and, as a result, a steady rhythm of success and momentum will have been achieved.

However, for newly launched businesses, building, and of course sustaining, momentum is a necessity and more often than not dictates the level of success for your company and its future growth and development. From my past experiences, momentum needs to be established within the early stages of starting up as the companies that strive for momentum immediately after they've opened their doors are the ones that will see considerable business growth within a much shorter length of time than those who are content with achieving the bare minimum.

Nevertheless, many small business owners fall into the trap of thinking momentum is something that should come at a later point in their career and, after exhausting all of their efforts to launch a business, feel they can reward themselves by taking a break as they feel the hard work is over. After exerting so much energy refining your idea, preparing a plan, securing funding and eventually launching your business, why wouldn't you want it to be a success immediately? Whilst it's important to reward yourself for your accomplishments and be able to step away from your company, simply starting a business is only half of the battle; it's moulding that business into a success that is the fully realised achievement.

All About IT
by Andy Hinxman

Director of Keybridge IT Solutions

There has been a revolution in IT in the last three years. It is called the Cloud. Where once all new businesses had to think about setting up and paying for servers, server rooms, cooling systems for server rooms, an army of technical staff to run server rooms and the ongoing maintenance costs, we can now set up and run our businesses in a much more cost efficient and effective way when it comes to IT.

If at the start you choose not to have an office, or simply want to work from home, your employees can access all they need through the Cloud. You can share and store information and pay for more storage as and when you need it.

When I started my own business in January 2011, I decided to go with a Cloud-based system because there wasn't much in terms of setup costs. Using the Cloud makes the most sense for businesses and start-ups as they grow. Microsoft now give away storage of 1TB per person and emails of up to 25GB in a mailbox costing as little as £2 per month. You just don't need systems/servers, etc., any more. There are also so many options for companies as they expand. You can pay for each individual or desk and then as you grow you pay to increase that number for things like IT support.

Naming the business

So many people come up with what they think is a great name for their company, only to find that the relevant domain has been taken. We chose Keybridge because it was the name of the first data centre suite in which we had servers. We then played around with the words – key stone, key rock – and came up with my favourite, which was Keybridge. I did try to buy the Keybridge domain from the company which owned it but they didn't want to sell. We then went for Keybridge IT, which made sense and also meant we could have that as our email address.

If you want your customers to find you, then check out the domain first. Be clear about your name. If you don't, you may end up with a domain and email so far removed from your company name that your customers struggle to find you.

Friendly help

When you start your own business, you will find yourself inundated with advice from well-meaning friends who want to help. Some of them may have some knowledge of IT and computer systems. Some of them will be happy to help you set up what they think you need. However, do be careful before you take them up on their offer. Trying to do everything as cheaply as possible at the start can have an impact in the long run. You could also end up losing your friends if things go wrong.

I have been called in to sort out some horrendous issues because friends that have been helping out with IT simply haven't been competent to deal with problems as and when they occur. It is better to take professional advice right from the start.

Even more damaging is when things go wrong. What recourse do you have to a friend if all your data is lost in six months' time, or if the friend doesn't have time to help you resolve your email issues? It is far better to have professional support with a service level agreement that you can rely on from the very beginning.

I would also recommend that you don't go for the quick and easy option of simply using a Yahoo or Hotmail account for your company email. You may be keen and want to get started as soon as possible, but ask yourself how professional it looks to have abc@hotmail.com. It doesn't have your company name and messages from this address could end up being caught in your client's spam filter.

Data back-up and security

So you have started to build your business and as you grow it is essential you are able to keep customer information safe – not just for you, but for them as well. Losing data can ruin a business. Think about it. If it is customer information used for sales, what will you do if you no longer have their contact details, prices and other relevant information? Or think about it from a legal point of view. What if that information is covered by the Data Protection Act? Protecting that data is crucial and it could be very expensive if it is lost or stolen.

Interestingly, I know some small businesses keep their company data on just one laptop. That includes everything from proposals to accounts, as well as important and often confidential information. A scary thought. Laptops can be lost or stolen. To a thief the laptop may simply be a quick and easy way of getting some cash. To the small business owner that laptop is worth much, much more than simply the cost of the machine.

I would recommend using the Cloud as a backup. It won't prevent your laptop from being stolen but it does mean you will have a backup of your important information. Don't forget to lock documents and information that is sensitive and confidential. That way, if the thief has an ulterior motive – e.g. wants to find out who your customers are, your bank account details, staff home addresses, etc. – they will be blocked from doing so.

Staff IT security

This is a tricky topic because as a start-up you may be close to your staff. You are most likely to be working in a small team and trust is crucial for any business to work. But consider the long term. People move on. They get other jobs. Those jobs may be with your competitors. They may set up on their own. There may be staff working for you who don't get on. It happens.

Rather than sharing whole folders, encourage staff to simply send over relevant documents. There may well be information in the full folder that you don't want everyone to read. The same applies when storing data on a server or in the Cloud. When done properly, you can allow only named individuals to have access to certain folders. A good example would be around finance. Do you want everyone in your company to be able to view and amend your accounts and payroll information?

If, like many companies, you give your employees access to company data via mobile devices, make sure you have the power to ask the individual to remove that account when they leave. If not, they walk away with the contacts, emails and other information. You should include data security in employee contracts and a clause to say that the company has the right to wipe devices before the employee leaves.

Cloud vs. server

There is no doubt, Cloud-based systems have revolutionised the way small businesses are able to make the best use of their IT systems. So long as you put in place security measures, as mentioned, then being able to allow staff to share documents and data whether they are at home or in the office is a great way to ensure continuity of business. It works well when many people work part of their week at home, when issues arise with the transport system, such as Tube strikes in London, or the rail network caught by a deluge of leaves on the line or snow. With some systems you can also move the shared files so they can be viewed on various devices, such as mobile phones and tablets, as well as computers. The options include Microsoft Office 365, Google Drive, or a Cloud hosting system.

Alternatively, to install a server would cost you around £2000. Then there are the ongoing maintenance and backup costs. With the Cloud, the systems grow with the business and there are no upfront costs. Not a cheery thought, but if your office was to burn down or be flooded, there is every chance the server could be damaged. That could put you out of business, not just for a few days but maybe entirely. At least if you are on the Cloud you can move staff to a temporary work hub or get them to work from home and your information and documents will all be safe.

Level of support

How important is IT to you? Could you run your business if you had no access to email or your documents for an hour, a day or a week? Depending on the answer to that question, you should make sure you have the necessary support in place just in case things go wrong. You can include that in the terms of service with your IT support.

Many companies, including Keybridge, offer remote support via services like LogMeIn. However, those services are of little use if you have serious software issues or if you have no internet, so don't underestimate the usefulness of engaging a company who are local to you, so they can come in and resolve any problems in person. Bear in mind too that the cheapest option may turn out to be the most expensive mistake you'll ever make – you get what you pay for.

Apprentices

I would advise anyone starting their own business is to take on apprentices. We've had four and they have all stayed on to become full-time employees. Apprentices are keen to learn how you and your business work, they come to you with no bad habits or preconceptions and you can train them in the way you want things done. The government helps fund apprentices, which is useful for start-ups in terms of budgeting for staff.

Planning for the future

It is exciting when your business starts to grow. I had many colleagues and ex-colleagues who wanted my help so it made sense for me to set up on my own. I'm looking forward to expanding and eventually getting into a position of being able to sell the business.

I understand the decisions you have to make when you are starting up. As a new business you can fall into the category of spending too much, or not enough, on your IT system. Don't think you need to take everything offered to you in terms of IT. Do ask for advice as there are a lot of options. Think carefully about what you actually **need** and make sure you can add to this as the business grows and changes.

A good IT system should give you support when you need it, reliable backup of all your data, and should grow with your business.

How To Go Global
by FedEx

The international opportunity

For the first time since 2007, things are looking up for the UK economy. As we move away from recession, there is rising optimism amongst businesses that a period of prosperity is on the horizon. Exporting is vital to this, as evidenced by the demanding government target of increasing exports to £1trn by 2020.

Our release of the *FedEx Great British Export Report* in 2014 comes at an important crossroads for the UK economy, and reveals an unspoken truth about the gap between popular opinion and what is happening on the frontline. It offers insight into what UK entrepreneurs really think about exporting, why so many are not currently doing so, and how these barriers can ultimately be overcome. In fact, a key finding was that only one quarter of UK SMEs are currently 'internationally active,' which shows there is still much more to be done.

The global view

The time is now for UK businesses to prepare for the internationalisation of their activities. This will allow them to get off to a flying start on the global stage and succeed in driving the UK economy forward, as long as they have access to the correct support required to help propel them to continuing international success.

Global trade is at the very heart of the FedEx business and our network is a critical enabler of the global supply chain. We believe that the growing and evolving global economy presents great opportunities for businesses worldwide, especially as the world is more connected than ever before.

We can harness this trend to strengthen our economic recovery, generate growth and create jobs. Global trade helps us to be globally competitive. Today, with access to the internet and access to globally enabled logistics providers, businesses can sell their goods and services to, and find their suppliers in, virtually any market around the world.

Global opportunities for UK business

In order to capitalise on the opportunities a global economy can provide, UK businesses need to look to export to international markets in 2014. According to the Confederation of British Industry, British businesses that do this are more than 10% more likely to succeed and survive than those that do not. In fact, many analysts argue there has never been a better time for UK businesses to look to foreign shores.

The UK market currently accounts for less than 1% of the global population so businesses who do not export abroad are missing huge opportunities to expand into new markets with new customers. The UK tends to export to more traditional and mature markets, but British businesses should also look to tap into markets further afield where demand outstrips supply. The shift toward a global-local-world is driven by the internet, as it gives businesses the potential to capture a global customer base. This is perhaps why the number of businesses actively exporting goods and services from the UK is slowly rising. Improvements in technology have also made exporting easier than ever, whilst next day-international delivery options have helped to remove the geographical and time limitations to entering overseas markets.

The Great British Export Report even found, of those companies which currently export, 41% predict that their activities will be mostly international in just five years, rising to 50% in 15 years. It seems the importance of international trade has been realised, but more businesses need to consider 'going global' in the near future, rather than looking further down the line.

How to navigate a global marketplace

Among UK businesses, there seems to be a lack of awareness – not to the benefits to exporting, but to the resources available, which are plentiful if you know where to look. Businesses also seem to be unsure of how to get started. The Great British Export Report 2014 in fact revealed the type of barriers SMEs face when it comes to accessing new markets, with 20% of companies surveyed reporting a lack of technical knowledge and a concern over the costs, whilst 14% were waiting for economic conditions to improve further.

At FedEx, we are experts in navigating the global marketplace, and as such we've put together a list of our top ten exporting 'Must Dos' to achieve exporting success.

1. **Keep an open mind.** Exporting to established economies may seem like the easy option, but don't forget that new markets are emerging all the time. You may already have considered selling to the Baltics, for example, but have you considered South Africa?

2. **Do your research.** Getting clued up on potential markets does not need to cost the earth. The internet is a brilliant resource as are small business groups and networks. Once you've identified a country, try to get out there and meet the locals, browse the supermarket shelves and shop windows to scope out the competition, and meet distributors face-to-face.

3. **Test the waters.** Focus on one country for starters to ensure your domestic business is kept in order. There's plenty of time to conquer the rest of the world!

4. **Be prepared.** In e-commerce, a product's popularity can go from nought to 100 incredibly quickly. Ensure you make plans just in case your product flies out of the blocks faster than you expect.

5. **Look for funding.** The government recognises the importance of exporting by offering £3 billion in funding to UK businesses. Make sure you take full advantage of this – your competitors might already be doing so.

6. **Consider your brand.** What works in the UK may not work abroad. Why not take advantage of the excellent reputation British products enjoy overseas by incorporating "British-ness" into your brand to give it the edge over its local counterparts?

7. **Ask: "Is the price right?"** Your product's perfect price point will differ from country to country, and getting it right is absolutely crucial to securing distributors and customers. Don't forget to factor in

additional transport costs and exchange rates to keep your margins healthy.

8. **Get accustomed to customs.** This is a crucial but often overlooked step when exporting. Customs regulations can vary a lot from country to country so check early in the process to find out if there are barriers to your product. This could save you a lot of time and effort.

9. **Think like a local.** Getting to grips with a new culture isn't just an enlightening personal experience, it's fundamental to the success of your product. In some places, haggling can make a deal, in others it can break one. Getting to know the local business culture helps you understand what makes the people tick, allowing harmonious and productive relationships to flourish.

10. **Logistics is a lot more than just A to B.** Whoever transports your goods overseas, make sure you tap into their expertise. The right logistics firm can offer you invaluable advice on navigating customs and give you an insight into which market may be right for you.

Let logistics be your compass

You may find it helpful to find a trusted global transportation provider. Logistics is so important because it is a solution for getting the right thing to the right place at the right time – and in the process bringing real value to your supply chain. Many express carriers not only satisfy your transport needs but also have integrated customs brokerage operations around the world, helping you to access new markets and revenue streams. A logistics provider is essential in helping you conquer new markets and build a higher level of compliance while you focus on your core business.

Case Study: Bremont

One such business that has benefitted from logistics support during its global expansion is the luxury watch company Bremont. Based in Oxfordshire, Bremont was founded by brothers Giles and Nick English. They spent five years developing their product before launching their first collection of highly developed aviation inspired timepieces in 2007.

Establishing a small business is challenging enough, let alone navigating the complexities of watchmaking in the hyper-competitive world of luxury goods. Nick and Giles were fortunate enough to get early help from Walpole, a UK-based small-business incubator that pairs up-and-coming luxury brands with mentors from British business. Nick and Giles were connected with Andrew Gosheron, vice president of Field Sales Europe, FedEx.

Importing watch components for handcrafting and then exporting finished watches internationally is a complex endeavour. With FedEx guidance, Nick and Giles were able to smoothly manage the customs process and turn their attention to customer service and delivery – critical for a luxury brand.

Bremont ships its high-end timepieces everywhere from Shanghai to San Francisco using FedEx International Priority®, which means it doesn't have to worry about customs holdups. Shipping in the UK is handled with FedEx Next Day, an overnight service that bolsters the Bremont brand's high-end image. For behind-the-scenes logistics, including creating labels and online billing, Bremont uses FedEx Ship Manager® (**fedex.com/gb**).

Bremont has a firm toehold in the Caribbean and the United Arab Emirates, especially in Dubai. It has also opened a second branded boutique in Hong Kong, and is now moving aggressively into the US by selling through a network of highly prestigious, independent retailers and building strategic brand partnerships.

Next steps

In summary, UK businesses cannot afford to turn away from global trade, and we cannot protect or insulate ourselves from the growing world economy. Businesses that want to be entrepreneurial should take this chance to expand, taking advantage of the dynamism and opportunities a global economy offers. Economic globalisation has revolutionised how businesses interact and the internet provides increased potential to capture a global customer base. Technological advancements in logistics, such as next day international delivery, have removed the geographical and time limitations to entering international markets, allowing British businesses to capitalise by selling their products abroad.

Global trade is at the very heart of the FedEx business., We believe that this is crucial in order to allow businesses to grow and evolve worldwide, as the world becomes increasingly interconnected.

Building Your Personal Brand
by Jessica Huie MBE

Serial entrepreneur and founder of ColorBlind Cards and JH Public Relations

"I do not believe you can do today's job with yesterday's methods and be in business tomorrow."

– Nelson Jackson, automobile pioneer

We are all walking, talking brands, often unintentionally. Perceptions of us are formed within moments based on our appearance, communication, network and associations, but beyond this superficial concoction it is our personal values which define this brand. Essential for successful leadership and sustained business success, a powerful personal brand strategy should not be replaced by an ill-thought-out, quick hit of self-promoting social media output. Rather, this should be viewed as an ongoing journey which underpins and authenticates the very foundation of our business and being.

In this online, virtual and wholly personal age, it is ill advised to hide behind our product or service, purely reliant on its brilliance to engage the consumer. The digital era demands transparency, and understanding and refining your personal brand before launching it on to the market will ensure you speak effectively to the target audience. This will enable them to resonate with your values and buy, quite literally, into your story. It need not be stagnant. Your personal brand should be viewed as an evolving asset and valued and respected as such.

It is personal branding which differentiates and distinguishes you from competitors, so view it as a simple PR and marketing exercise at your peril – indeed it is your brand which should inform those channels and not vice versa. Personal branding is not cosmetic, it should be your truth.

The global financial crash signalled a watershed as damaged corporate reputations and the revelation of ethical lapses in business cleared the way for a new era – and a change in the way we do business forever. Out went a purely economic focus and in came corporate social responsibility, casting a spotlight on the individuals who yield power, their morals and motivation. Accountability was introduced.

Align personal and business values

Today the most successful brands with longevity have aligned personal and business values which create authenticity, trust and dependability. This is an appealing combination the consumer audience can buy into and resonate with. Consumers are more savvy, spoilt for choice due to the depth of an overpopulated marketplace. Our spending habits have changed and we are no longer motivated purely by our wants and needs – consumers expect a broader insight into businesses, which the digital era has made possible. One by one brands built on a disingenuous foundation have crumbled. Los Angeles Clippers boss Donald Sterling's PR nightmare serves as a perfect example.

The National Basketball Association (NBA) is built on African-American players. At last count in 2013, 76% of NBA players were African-American, but at the top of the food chain just 2% of the NBA's majority owners are black. If we look specifically at the Clippers, ten out of twelve of the team players are black men, and yet off the pitch Sterling's comments to his girlfriend that it bothered him that she would "associate with black people" and that he would prefer she did not bring them to his games, caused a global outcry and ultimately saw him fined $2.5 million and banned from the NBA for life.

The equally notorious old tale of entrepreneur Gerald Ratner, who denounced his own jewellery as "crap" and wiped £500 million from the value of his stores overnight, also serves as a prime example of dire personal branding. The fallout in both benchmark cases, where the true value system and mindset of these business owners was revealed, resulted in irreconcilable commercial and credibility brand damage.

The irony about life is that the truth will at some point reveal itself, and even those self aware enough to recognise the disconnect between their personal values and the pretence of their business values cannot fail to be exposed. There is no compensation for authenticity, and audiences can see through branding messages that do not correlate to behaviour.

Times and business have changed, the value systems and ethics of major players are up for examination like never before. Our love for Apple and Virgin is contributed to by the fact that we celebrate and buy into the drive, passion and genius of Richard Branson and the late Steve Jobs.

If you are a business owner, putting a face to your brand can be a powerful PR tool, but before you step centre stage be sure to self-critique. When a brand's rhetoric is not aligned with the customer's experience, integrity falters and trust is lost.

It is a personal brand that investors will buy into, have confidence in, and which post-exit provides the foundation for new business exploits and positive notoriety. Branson, Dyson, Gates, Winfrey are all perfect examples of leadership enabled through authentic personal branding. Respect, influence and a strong reputation are the return on the investment in a strong personal brand.

Consumers take confidence in brands transparent enough to own their values, deliver what they say they will, sincerely be who they are and communicate that brand promise. Ultimately it is about having an engaging, honest story and committing to deliver what you promise.

Defining your personal story

So how to identify the asset that is your human interest story? Our values are the sum of our experiences and journey, our personal story. If you genuinely believe that your business adds value to your customers' lives, then it's important to communicate that personally. By being visible rather than relying on your faceless brand to sell itself, you allow your customers the opportunity to understand the ethos behind your brand and your business values, and if you are marketing to the right audience then your values will resonate with them and make them more likely to buy.

Define and refine your personal story by asking yourself what the inspiration behind your business was; what is your vision? How are you improving, changing or distributing that which will benefit your audience? Give your customers an insight into the entrepreneur behind the business through your PR and marketing material and witness how effective this approach can be. Understanding your personal brand will help you to identify your competitive position as you understand what makes you stand out and how you add value. Are you traditional, mainstream or niche? Are you an expert authority?

Personal branding begins the moment we enter a room or engage in conversation, but to build that brand so that you become an influencer requires six basic steps. Following these will help to position you as the go-to individual within your field.

1. Establish your area of expertise

Experts come in different guises. There are those whose training and academia equips them to speak from a position of expertise, and those whose experiences and life journey make them compelling and inspiring to learn from. Often expertise is a combination of the two.

2. Create a content distribution strategy

From a digital perspective this means keywords pertinent to your expertise must be implemented into the content you distribute online through opinion articles, blogs and columns for business publications. By doing this, when somebody searches for a topic which falls under your expert area, you help to ensure that your name or company is visible.

3. Speak to your audience

Identify who your audience are so that you can communicate effectively with a sector who share your values and will be receptive to your expertise and experience. Whether you are speaking publicly or communicating through copy, remember that *you* are the product and regardless of the platform, you will be selling yourself.

4. Capitalise on your brand

Nothing adds kudos and instant gravitas like a book. In the absence of a physical hard copy publication, eBooks are a great tool for sharing expertise. Once you have cemented your thought leadership through a dedicated effort to follow these steps, your reputation will make it far easier for you to garner the interest of a book publisher.

5. Develop your public speaking skills

If you are serious about public speaking and want to consider agency representation – such as through JH Public Relations – consider that we will take into account whether you are knowledgeable in your field, whether you will be a draw for an audience and whether you have the skills to deliver an enjoyable presentation. I strongly recommend you consider some outside training for speaking if it is something you intend to pursue seriously.

6. Invest in PR

Finally, your personal brand is redundant if you remain unknown to your audience. Incorporate PR into your marketing strategy to support your content distribution. Ensure the key industry trade titles within your sector are aware of you by sharing useful content for their publications. Broadcast media provides a powerful medium for raising your profile and the ultimate aim is to be the name on everybody's lips to provide comment when a topic within your remit hits the headlines.

* * *

When we set aside the commercial benefits of a great personal brand, what we are really talking about is the desire for integrity and the authentic benefits which come from operating professionally with honesty. We often over-complicate business with jargon, but when all is said and done, letting our actions reflect our words and ensuring our service or product delivers on its promise, is the foundation for a brand success no marketing strategy, advertising or PR stunt can compensate for.

"Authentic brands don't emerge from marketing cubicles or advertising agencies. They emanate from everything the company does."

– Howard Schultz, Starbucks CEO

The Business Case for International Trade

by Samuel Kasumu and Elizabeth Adeniran

Founder, EN Campaigns; Enterprise Development Manager, EN Campaigns

Developing a growth strategy often arouses great debate within an organisation. For a start-up this is more of a challenge as most are one-man businesses and any growth strategy they wish to implement will need to be adapted as the company grows and evolves. Key questions arise in the process: do you simply sell the same product in the same market, sell the same product in a new market, or do you instead re-engage current customers with a different product entirely? There are no uniform answers and every business must assess their resources and capabilities as well as the opportunities that any given market could potentially present. To put it simply, businesses must have an emergent strategy that adapts to the changing business environment.

Large businesses often get complacent with their emergent strategy. A lot of businesses have fallen on tough times because they have failed to develop a clear growth strategy during the good times, often relying too much on a customer or a group of customers. These same customers in turn move on, enticed by something new and different, or adapting to changes in their personal circumstances.

A present example would be the challenges that supermarket chains are facing with the rise of discount retailers such as Lidl and Aldi. The latter has won numerous awards, if the TV ads are anything to go by: Quality Food Awards 2013 and the Grocer Gold Award are just two of these. You could argue that the likes of Tesco were too fixed on their current model and their market analysis only accounted for technological changes as opposed to a potential cultural shift. They have now found themselves locked in price wars with the discount supermarkets.

International diversification

Businesses must be one step ahead if they are to survive. One of the principle strategies that ensure they remain competitive and sustainable is diversification. Large companies have often diversified by setting their sights abroad. For example, Diageo has developed into a multinational powerhouse as a result of a broader horizon. For sport lovers, the Premier League has been a strong example of how a company can export its product across the world to significantly increase revenues. Unfortunately, it is usually the larger corporations that have chosen international expansion as a route to expansion and diversification.

For too many UK SMEs, quite often growth choices are confined to the domestic markets within which they currently operate. However, my opinion has always been that all of the businesses I am involved in must focus on an inevitable expansion into a new country or countries from the start. When developing our strategic plan we have the foreign markets we will be targeting directly in mind, which often helps us plan ahead.

There is a perception that doing business abroad can often be expensive, challenging and risky, but I would argue that quite often the rewards far outweigh any hurdles that need crossing. The opportunity to experience business and cultures in some of the most fascinating countries is something that any entrepreneur simply needs to ensure they have made the most of.

Why should an SME look outside of its domestic country of operation? For me the answer is very simple: opportunity. Currently only one-in-five British SMEs export overseas, but UKTI figures show that SMEs who export are 34% more likely to be productive in their first year of operations than those who do not. They are also 11% more likely to survive if they export. Further research conducted by UKTI shows that exporting has a positive impact on business productivity, with 85% of businesses who export saying it led to unexpected levels of growth.

The UK has a relatively small population compared to other larger markets, it has limited natural resources, and despite some positive growth post-recession, its annual growth levels are less attractive compared to many other markets. All in all, there are new players challenging the traditional developed markets.

What markets to target

Once you have tackled the why question, the next thing to reflect on will be which countries to target. It can be argued that emerging markets present the best options for most businesses. We can take Barclays as an example of a company that has recently realised emerging economies must be at the heart of its growth. Whilst announcing 19,000 job losses over the next three years, the chief executive also announced the company's renewed focus on Africa as a key growth area. "We're in the top 10 in Africa, we've got to get to the top five," Stephen van Coller, head of Absa Capital, the Johannesburg-based investment bank of Barclays Africa Group Ltd (BGA), said. "Trading and investment banking very much has an African focus now."

The type of product or service will often determine which nations present the best opportunities. Let's look at a few SMEs. WhoSounds saw the FIFA World Cup as an opportunity to expand and increase revenue. WhoSounds specialises in customised Bluetooth speakers, featuring *Dr Who*, *Spider-Man*, *Star Wars* and *Iron Man* designs. To coincide with the World Cup, they used their resources of specialised colours and designs to create speakers for flags, which have no copyright infringement. During the tournament they saw nine countries take up orders of between 2,000 and 3,000 units at an RRP of £49.99.

Tangle Teezer is another SME. Founder Shaun Pulfrey says: "I've seen business growth first hand. I started Tangle Teezer six years ago and we're now exporting to countries from the Netherlands (this was our first market) to China." China, their largest market, sees 300 orders per day. "There are 260 million Chinese consumers who shop online, and you can manage the whole of this huge market from a desk in the UK. They love the 'Made in the UK' stamp."

Still thinking about the issue of which countries to expand to, let's take the emerging markets of the BRICS nations (Brazil, Russia, India, China and South Africa) as an example. For the past 15 years these countries have driven global growth at unprecedented levels. Emerging markets accounted for more than half of global GDP growth over that period. China and India alone in 2013 accounted for 20% of world GDP. The BRICS have launched their own bank and are pressing ahead with the objective of overtaking established Western markets in the not too distant future. The BRICS have a total population of 2.8 billion, which is approximately 40% of the world's total. With a growing middle class and an increasing disposable income, this presents an opportunity to new companies to tap into these markets. With many businesses having the potential to be conducted online, there has never been a better time to embrace the 'Made in Britain' tag.

More interesting than the BRICS for me are a set of countries that Goldman Sachs named the *Next 11*. These are countries that are just beginning to realise their economic potential and could in fact become even more powerful than their BRICS neighbours. Take for example Nigeria. This is the most populous country in Africa and recently overtook one of the BRICS, South Africa, as the number one economy in Africa. Not only does Nigeria have access to more natural resources than South Africa, but it also has a larger population, access to relatively cheap labour and a financial services industry that is on the up. The country is currently dealing with the issue of terrorism, however this is largely concentrated within the northern region which is quite a distance from the financial and oil districts.

Practicalities of trading

Let's now move on to look at how you trade once you have identified the markets you wish to expand into. There are a number of ways to conduct research, including the internet at the very basic level, but also through engagement directly through trade associations like the British Chamber of Commerce. There are also opportunities to engage with trade missions; these give you the chance to network with potential clients and will help to give a better understanding of the various challenges that must be overcome to start business within a respective country. **ExportBritain. org.uk** is a site that publicises some trade missions.

UKTI are perhaps the most underutilised tool available to British companies seeking to do business abroad. They employ over 2000 business advisors, have established offices within many countries, and often have relationships with key stakeholders within regions. There are also a number of grants available for those seeking to explore opportunities abroad.

After initial research and possible trade missions there comes the time to consider how exactly to start. Having a local partner is perhaps the best way to start a business and often helps to save some of the costs associated with opening a business as a foreign company. A local partner will be able to deal with any cultural challenges and will have the advantage of helping to accelerate growth. Of course there are challenges when seeking to identify partners that can be trusted and are credible, which is where utilising the skills of the likes of UKTI is useful.

In addition to having local partners, it often helps to have staff members based in the UK with links to the country where a business seeks to operate. Employing people from communities that have dual nationalities often helps to give businesses a competitive advantage, particularly when seeking to operate in non-English speaking nations. The reality is that whilst English remains the global language of business, the developing countries where opportunities are most attractive are not traditionally English speaking. For instance, Chinese Mandarin is listed by UNESCO as the most spoken language in the world by native and second language speakers. Language barriers can often slow down negotiations and logistical planning, especially when needing to employ local staff or establish an office.

Looking to the future

What is clear is that Britain's future as a major player in the increasingly global business environment could be at risk if we continue to believe that only the very largest firms should operate internationally. SMEs must be brave and engage with foreign markets as they could find unparalleled growth opportunities which will create jobs at home and abroad. We have been left behind by businesses from other nations that have been more willing to travel and more proactive in engaging new markets.

For businesses to successfully trade we need to ask the question of what it is we can trade well with in the first place. Financial services are a key export area for Britain due to our excellent reputation globally. We are also making significant progress in financial technology, an area where Britain has been leading the way in recent times. The UK economy is becoming increasingly dynamic as technology helps to reintroduce Britain into the world of innovation. The challenge for other business areas is how we compete with countries with lower labour costs and a better understanding of the cultures within emerging markets.

The prime minister has stated that he plans to increase UK exports to £1trn by 2020. There have been many success stories, including skincare brand Bulldog, whose oversees business has grown to £2 million and 30% of its overall revenues. Another is tea company Tregothnan, which has recently expanded into China following a successful trade mission. It went on to have an official launch event hosted by UKTI, with over 40 key stakeholders present, and had a documentary aired to over 600 million viewers across China.

All entrepreneurs from Great Britain must have a global growth perspective in order to truly achieve significant growth and spread the risks that come from being heavily reliant on one customer and/or marketplace.

Paperless – or Just Smarter Printing?

by John Gifford

OKI business manager for managed document services

Businesses have been talking about the paperless office for decades. Ask anyone to describe their idea of the office of the future and it's likely to be stark, minimalist and totally free of paper. Yet, somehow, this ideal for tomorrow's world hasn't arrived, even in today's age of electronic documents and communications.

Many companies have a clear desk policy and organisations such as the NHS have set goals to go paperless by a certain date in order to become greener, more efficient and save billions of pounds of taxpayers' money. However, even with these targets in place, it's more likely that these organisations will remain paper light than paperless.

There are many reasons for this. For a start, until today's digital natives reach old age, there will always be someone who wants to write a letter or take notes with pen and paper. There are also some occasions when only a hard copy of a document is acceptable – for legal reasons, for example.

But there are also many organisations where use of paper is totally out of control – and many businesses don't actually know how much paper they use or how much they spend on printing. This is especially remarkable after a period of recession, when other resources have been pared down to the bone. It's unlikely that small to medium-sized businesses have a better idea of this than large corporates – in OKI's experience, paper and printing costs tend to be ignored by businesses of all sizes when it comes to cutting down on overheads.

It's also clear that, in many cases, this disregard runs through every level of an organisation. When OKI asked more than 2000 office workers across all industry sectors about their printing practices, 92% said that they still print at least one document every day. This is perhaps predictable – but more worrying is the fact that 45% print more than ten pages a day. A significant 15% print out more than 50 pages on an average day in the office.

The top reason given for this (64%) was the importance of the document and the need for hard copy evidence (54%). Presumably, in many sectors this reflects tightening regulations and the need for compliance. However, this hardly accounts for printing 50 or more pages daily. Likewise, perhaps it's not too surprising that 79% use office equipment to print personal documents, but what is concerning is that 9% claim to do this at least once a day.

While not suggesting that companies suddenly stop workers printing what they need to, it would benefit them to take better control by first auditing exactly how much printing is being done and how much paper is used, and adopting and managing a print strategy. In the same poll, only 27% said that their company had such a policy in place that was being actively enforced. Nearly half, 47%, admitted that they had no such policy.

Cutting printing volumes

There are several small measures that can drastically cut paper volumes – for example, ensuring that double-sided mono print is the default option for everyday work. This is an easy and logical step and yet it's surprising how many companies neglect to take it.

Beyond this, it may pay small businesses in the long run to get expert help. This needn't be expensive as vendors such as OKI offer managed print and document services. This takes the pressure away from capital expenditure budgets as services are paid for on a monthly basis and everything is taken care of with one contract, including guidance, supplies, maintenance and support.

Printers have moved on by leaps and bounds in the last couple of years. On the other hand, older devices tend to waste paper when runs get jammed or there are imperfections in the end result. Consequently, advice from the experts will help assess current printers and investigate the ROI on new models which waste less paper, are energy-efficient and run smoothly.

It's a case of using the right printer for the job. For example, replacing multiple desktop printers and scanners with a smaller number of multifunction printers can be hugely cost-effective. Many of these new multifunction devices come with an open platform enabling the customisation of the user interface to integrate all document-related tasks into an organisation's document workflow. This will enable a paper-free document flow, such as scan or fax to email, where a scanned image is automatically converted to a PDF and emailed directly to someone's inbox.

Some printers enable users to store documents prior to printing on the printer's hard disk drive or secure data card. This means that these are only converted to paper when needed and the security of confidential information is improved.

Again, as part of a managed services approach, multifunction printers also deliver advanced security features, including secure PIN printing, data encryption and disk wiping, plus a secure print with card release option. These provide peace of mind that sensitive documents won't get into the wrong hands.

Working closely with a managed document services provider will help put all these changes in place. When documents and printing are managed more carefully and expertly, paperless becomes less of an issue.

Case study: Homes for Northumberland

Homes for Northumberland is responsible for the management of over 8500 homes on behalf of Northumberland County Council. The company deployed 55 printing devices from a broad range of vendors. These were scattered across its Blyth headquarters, a site in Alnwick and its Blyth stores depot to support its intensive requirement for general office and administrative printing.

Many of these printers were aging without a maintenance contract in place and the company found that the process of carrying out general repairs to the printers was consuming too much in-house IT resource. The sheer number of printers and the fact that they came from multiple vendors meant that managing stocks of consumables was an expensive and unwieldy process.

Homes for Northumberland decided to look for a single supplier, capable of taking over all responsibility for supply, service and consumables for copy, print, fax and scanning requirements at a fixed cost per print. It also began to look at the possibility of investing in a managed document services solution. Following an analysis of volumes printed by Homes for Northumberland's existing printing solutions fleet, OKI proposed a managed document services solution, designed to improve printing efficiency and productivity. OKI calculated that this would involve a 42% reduction in devices, while providing more multifunction printers to facilitate the growing need for scanning and copying of documents.

Homes for Northumberland now pays for its printing resource on a cost per page basis, which incorporates costs for toner supply, repair and maintenance to the printers, saving the company money and making budgeting more predictable. It also acts as an inflation buster, with the cost per page kept constant for a five-year period.

The managed document services approach frees up the time of the company's IT services and support team, which no longer needs to carry out printer maintenance. Typically, it also means less printer downtime, as an engineer can be on site the next day if there are any problems. In addition, OKI provides a customer help desk for issues that can be resolved over the phone. By reducing the overall size of the fleet from 55 devices, including printers, copiers and fax machines, down to 29, Homes for Northumberland has been able to significantly reduce the volume of expensive toner stock it has to keep. Now it simply phones OKI for new consumables whenever it needs them.

The company also gains major benefits from the functionality of the printers themselves. The new printers are highly energy efficient, which helps keep running costs low. Also, the new multifunction printers have provided capabilities that it did not have previously, such as scanning a document to email, or it can send an incoming fax to a PC or a network folder.

Keeping up with mobile

One reason why many companies may suddenly find a drop in paper use is the increasing presence of tablets and smartphones in business –

and the trend towards bring your own device, or BYOD. While positive in one way – because difficulties in printing from these devices may cut unnecessary printing – this can also produce inefficiencies for the opposite reason when hard copies are genuinely needed. Going back to the OKI survey, almost half (49%) of those polled said that they either can't print at all in their office using their own smartphone or tablet, or that the printer is supposed to be enabled, but still presents a challenge when trying to print from a mobile device.

This is another area where a managed services partner can advise on the right path to take. Many affordable printers are now Cloud-connected which means that users can wirelessly print documents from any mobile phone, laptop, PC or other web-connected device. Mobile devices can find printers via a mobile app – for example, Google Cloud Print integrates with Chrome, Gmail for mobile and Google Docs for mobile – and can also print to third-party native mobile apps on Android and iOS platforms.

iPhone and iPad users can take advantage of Apple's AirPrint as this is embedded natively in these devices. This means that instead of having to transfer a document to the app itself, users can print directly from wherever the document or image is stored. Icons within the device will inform them whether there are any AirPrint-enabled printers in the vicinity.

The world of mobile printing is currently evolving fast and working with a managed print or document services provider can ensure that solutions take the latest advances into account.

Design features

Another area where having an expert partner combined with the latest printer models can really help a business is in optimising software within the printer for design purposes. Although this won't exactly help the paperless or paper-light cause, it will help a smaller business cut costly, outsourced printing by producing their own marketing and promotional materials in-house.

Sales and marketing collateral, including signs, labels, presentations, flyers and brochures, can be produced in-house. And business cards, letterheads, compliments slips and invoices can be given a consistent look and feel, reinforcing the company brand.

It seems that at the moment every aspect of business life is changing fast. For a small business focusing on getting started and making a profit, it can be difficult to keep up with the latest developments in technology. As a result, it's easy to miss out and – in the case of printers and printing – end up paying more than necessary, thanks to wasted paper, energy costs and not using the latest devices. Working with a managed print or document services partner can change all this and ensure that this aspect of the business, at least, is taken care of by the experts.

Plan to Get Lucky?
by Paul Samrah

Partner, Kingston Smith

"My business plan was to get lucky, and I did; that was great. And then my second business plan was to get lucky again, and there, I faltered."

– Val Kilmer

I'm amazed how many UK SMEs have business plans (two-thirds, give or take). I would imagine that, as an entrepreneur, you'd be so busy running around getting excited about your next venture that everything else could wait. Entrepreneurs are the kind of people you meet at the bar, have a five-minute chat with and, before you know it, your wife/husband/dog is standing by your side wondering where you've been for the last hour. They are interesting! That's why it's surprising that two-thirds of them have a written business plan.

What's not surprising is how many business owners write a plan and never look at it again. They expect it to just happen.

This chapter will be of great use for those who need to write a business plan. If you already have one, it'll be a good reminder of why you wrote it in the first place.

Why am I doing this?

A business plan is a blueprint; it's your road map to the future success of your business. The plan is an explanation and summary of your medium to long-term strategy. It explains the reasons for your business' activities, your future goals and plans to reach them, and the business' strengths, weaknesses, opportunities and threats – and how they are exploited and mitigated. Very helpful at 10pm on a Sunday night when you're wondering why you started this in the first place!

A business plan is not just an annotated profit & loss account. Nor is it a fairy tale scenario of good news with better and better news to come! It should be a coherent and balanced presentation which takes into account the realistic goals and needs of the business, normally for a period of time.

The quality that entrepreneurs and Val Kilmer have in common is positivity. Positive people are generally lucky, and if as a business owner you do see yourself as lucky, then the need for a plan can slip down the priority list. Indeed, why write a plan when you are doing so well in the first place? Well, because your luck will eventually run out and, as the saying goes, fail to prepare, prepare to fail.

Enough of the lecture; what are you going to do about it?

Here are some key things to consider when writing a business plan. Some you may have thought of, some may not even have been considered. If you answer the questions below, keep a record, commit to it and refer back to it; then you will be waving your competitors goodbye.

The basics

Who prepares the plan? You do! The business owner. You will need input from other stakeholders, such as your staff, your investors perhaps, your clients of course and even your accountant... I've heard they're good with numbers. This is going to give you a rounded view on your position in the market, your support and your financial aspirations. If this seems like a lot of work, use technology to help and send out a simple questionnaire to gather this information. SurveyMonkey offers this service for free.

Who benefits? Everyone! Management commitment increases during the preparation of the business plan and an uplift in staff morale is generated as the direction and the future of the business becomes clear. It's important that an abridged version is disseminated to staff to help them understand the needs of the business and where they fit in – why write a marvellous business plan and then hide it? The worst thing you can do is tell someone to do something without telling them why they are doing it.

SITREP (situation report – right here, right now)

First assess your current situation; prepare an old favourite – a SWOT analysis.

You could ask each staff member to do this; you might end up with something you hadn't thought of. Remember, strengths and weakness are internal – for example, high employee morale, abundance of talent, understaffing, and lack of internal processes. Opportunities and threats, on the other hand, are external – for example, a competitor folds and your market share increases, there's a fire in your warehouse, or you suffer industrial action.

You should include here a very brief history of your business, your mission statement, values and approach, the services and/or products you offer, and, essentially, the reason why the business exists.

Do include financials here, but obviously remove the sensitive information when distributing the abbreviated version.

And don't forget, this can all be in bullet points; it's not required to write your answer to *War and Peace*.

Products and services

List your products and services, along with their features, pricing, positioning, etc. Better still, use the 7Ps!

Product	What are you offering? What developments do you have on the horizon?
Price	A product or service is only worth what someone will pay for it. Too expensive and your customers will expect augmentation to the product or added value; charge too little and your product could be perceived as cheap.
Place	Is your product being sold in the right place? From a shop? Do you go to them? More often than not, it's online. How easy are you to find online? If you appear low down in the Google search rankings, say goodbye to revenue.
Promotion	Where do you get your business from? Referrals? From organic internet searches? Why not offer a reward scheme? Then invest in SEO.

People	Nowadays, customers buy a service as well as a product. Do your staff need training? Are they motivated?
Process	It's simple – systems create consistency and efficiency.
Physical evidence	This is especially important if you are providing an intangible service. This element gives customers something to touch, to remember you by, be it a 1980s stress ball, a brochure, or a framed picture of you.

This exercise should give you many answers and much inspiration for how to beat the competition.

Competitor analysis

There are several ways to analyse the competition. If you don't have an industry standard or league table then this can be very subjective. You could pay for a benchmarking service against your competitors (most business advisers should offer this). At the very least it would be wise to plot a competitor radar chart (like the one below). Choose the most important things for your business success and plot yourself against your competitors in these areas.

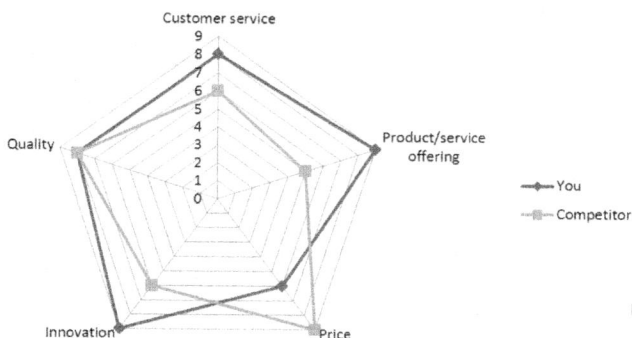

Competitor analysis is not a fast process; you will need to use several sources of information. Quite simply, the best and fastest way to keep up-to-date with it is by networking. You can talk to clients about what else is on the market, meet suppliers of competitors, meet competitors themselves – and all at the same time as mopping up some new business.

Marketing plan

Having analysed your current situation, your products and services, your competitors, and considered all of the other fantastic information you have collated, the marketing plan is by far the most exciting stage! Well, it is for me anyway.

Your marketing plan should contain KPIs (your key performance indicators), which will join your other business goals in your executive summary.

A KPI, or goal, needs to be SMART:

- specific
- measureable
- attainable
- realistic
- timely.

For example: *To achieve a 20% increase in revenue from product A by January 2015.*

Once you have written your KPIs you will need to produce a communication plan or Gantt chart to achieve these goals. This will include a list of all the activities, the resources you need (e.g. money and manpower), the deadline, and who is responsible for each activity.

Operations and management

The operations and management plan will help you understand how the business will function on a continuing basis. It will highlight the logistics of the organisation, such as the various responsibilities of the management team, the tasks assigned to each division within the business, and capital and expense requirements related to its operations.

Detail your proposed organisational structure using an organogram and identify training needed in order to deliver your business plan. Identify any potential recruitment requirements now and plan ahead.

Financial factors

Always keep on top of your financials, or engage an accountant to do this. You'll know if you've been successful in this because your balance sheet will be a beautiful thing.

If you think you are going to need additional finance to achieve your great plan, then look around. Bank lending is not always the best source of funding; crowdfunding and factoring could be good options instead. Finding the right type of finance for your business needs is important – it is definitely worth taking advice from your accountant on this.

Executive summary

Summarise your business plan in one to two paragraphs and pop this at the beginning of your document. This will remind you at a glance what you're aiming for. It will also assist any new members of the team who join after you have prepared your business plan.

Finally

A business plan is a working document. I cannot stress enough that you need to keep this updated throughout the year. Your competitor folds? Update your plan. You launch an unexpected and new product? Update your business plan. Your key salesperson leaves (hopefully not for a competitor)? Then update your business plan!

If you review your business plan as frequently as you can, I guarantee that you will have more direction, be more likely to achieve your goals, and depend less on luck – so that you don't crash and burn, Maverick (couldn't resist).

Bonus – tips for business planning bliss

- **Integrated financials:** The profit-and-loss account, balance sheet and cash flow forecast should be integrated. Link the cells between the statement spreadsheets to enable them to change in conjunction with each other. This will save time in the long run when you update the figures.

- **Presentation of projections:** Projections should cover no more than a three-year time frame. Highlights should be included in your business plan, with the detailed financials attached as an appendix.

- **Starting point:** If the business has already traded, the starting point of the projections must agree with the financial position of the business at that date. The starting cash position must agree with the bank reconciliation.

- **Assumptions:** List all your assumptions, based on evidence where possible. These should be linked to the model, so that when changed the model can be immediately changed.

- **Fantasy:** Don't be over-optimistic – you must be able to justify your projections.

- **Taxation:** Include a tax charge/credit calculation in your projections; provide for a research & development tax credit if appropriate.

- **Sensitivities:** Set up your projections so that best, expected and worst-case scenarios can be run through the model.

- **Key performance indicators (KPIs):** Develop KPIs that are relevant to your business and explain them in your plan.

- **Executive summary:** Give a brief overview of the concept's most important aspects, clearly, compellingly and concisely. The quality of this summary will determine whether the rest of the business plan is read.

Improving Our Lives
by Craig Goldblatt

Leadership speaker and coach

So much of life is still a mystery! We live in a world of such extremes – environmentally, physically, socially, spiritually, and of course financially. The world is changing at such a pace, but there are still things that seem to stay the same:

- our need to love and be loved

- to have a reason for living

- to know who we are and what's important to us

- to share our lives with others

- to feel that we have contributed in some way to our micro and macro community.

I have spent the last 11 years studying many people from all different walks of life, from remote tribes in the Amazon forest, to Sub-Saharan communities in West Africa while in Burkina Faso with Giving Africa, a charity I founded in 2010 (**www.givingafrica.org**).

Throughout the last decade of research I have uncovered a large number of different strategies for change. To me there is one framework that stands out above all others – Dilts' Neurological levels of change. During this chapter I have chosen this as a platform to explore how we can consistently improve the quality of our lives. Within this model there are six levels which greatly impact how we live.

Our **purpose**, our reason for being on the planet, directly impacts the quality of our **identity**, who we are at our very best as an individual.

This then shapes our **values and beliefs**, what's most important to us. These values create the confidence and clarity for us to take on more **capabilities and skills**, which is how we demonstrate our abilities to ourselves and others, and helps us to develop **behaviours** to aid what we do in our lives. This allows us to build empowering **environments** in which to live!

There are many different ways in which these key components could be described. What follows is my own way of expressing my experiences and life through the model.

My aim is that this will give you a footing from where you can do the same.

Purpose

As human beings, purpose is something that runs so deep. Those of us who connect to our true purpose on a regular basis draw so much power from this feeling of clarity. It is surely worth the challenging and emotional lifelong journey to find out our reason for being here.

At a physical level, we understand that we are here to reproduce and then to play a part in the natural evolution of the earth's ecosystem.

However, at a spiritual level we tend to express our purpose through personal experience and deep feelings of knowing. Some powerful examples of this are to love ourselves and our family, to grow our business, to give to our community, to serve our country and to create freedom for all.

To me our reason exists in every moment we're alive. As we travel through our lives there are times when we tap into this profound level of congruence. Through meditation and being present we are given the opportunity to experience more of our deepest purpose whilst we are on this earth.

Question: What is your reason for living and how are you living your purpose for you and all those that you love and share your life and business with?

Identity

We know that we have evolved over millions of years. Many ecological and natural changes have taken place. More recently our nationalities, tribes, clans, cultures, communities, families, and even our symbiotic relationships, have shaped us to become 21st century global citizens. Today we are unique, magnificent and complex beyond measure. We are part of something so large.

We believe we use only a small percentage of our internal resources, yet we continue to change, learn and grow at such a speed.

We create many powerful archetypes with which to share who we truly are – a father, mother, lover, child, fighter and friend. These words are now synonymous with our identity. Isn't it wonderful that the **more we learn, the more we realise there is still so much to know?**

Question: Who are you when you are at your very best?

Values

Shaped by our purpose and identity, we have a very strong emotional compass that sits deep within our hearts – often we refer to this as our core values. Again, we have created a list of strong meaningful words that help us to stay on track, to live our truth. Just a few examples of this are: health, honesty, integrity, passion, loyalty, fun, determination, empathy and compassion. It is said that these values have an inextricable link to our beliefs – the rules within our minds.

When we live our values through our beliefs to a very high level, the outcome is strength and a great level of self-confidence for us as individuals, for our teams and our whole organisation.

Question: What is most important to you in your life right now?

Skills

We now live our day-to-day lives with such pinpoint precision.

In this, the 21st century, there is of course a great sophistication to how we do things. We travel in planes, trains and cars at super speed and in great comfort; deliver products across the world in no time at all; we design computer games that seem so real; we communicate to our friends across the world in less than a second; serve a tennis ball at over 140 miles per hour; run 100 metres in under ten seconds; free dive to over 200 metres.

We have accomplished so much. They say that 10,000 hours of purposeful practice makes us a master. Learn what you have a passion for and always follow your heart. Not only will you become skilful, but you will absolutely love all that you do.

Question: How do you demonstrate your abilities to yourself and others?

Behaviour

What we demonstrate to others gives us an opportunity to learn in every moment of our lives. Our actions communicate our feelings and thoughts. Here is a great quote from Victor Frankl, which I believe teaches a great deal:

> "Between stimulus and response there is a space. In that space is our power to choose our response. And in our response lies our very growth and our freedom."

For me it is the intention behind the behaviour that counts, not the behaviour itself! In our businesses and personal lives, can we find out why people act in such a way before we choose to judge them?

Question: How do you demonstrate what you do to others?

Environment

Seven billion of us now share this small planet. As we all strive to grow our businesses and our mega-cities, some would say that we humans are damaging the earth beyond repair. I'm not so sure. In evolutionary terms we will surely only be present on this planet for the blink of an eye. Mother Nature often seems to find a way of fighting back with some force!

Having said this, we clearly have a profound financial, social and environmental responsibility to our children, to give them a chance to live and enjoy this extremely rich ecosystem. Where we live, work, play, learn and travel is transforming as we speak – from the smallest butterfly to the biggest whale, from the Manhattan skyline to the media city in Dubai, from the heart of the Amazon rainforest to the Australian outback.

We now have so many different environments to choose from. For me, the key is to be very proactive in the choice of where I live and spend my time. So often we try our best to hide our emotions to both ourselves and then others. This to me is taking away our opportunity to live our life as it is meant to be lived. There is a wonderful quote that shares how important it is in life to give everything and show everyone our real self, no matter how scary:

> "You've never lived until you've almost died. For those who have fought for it, life has a flavour the protected shall never know."
>
> – **Guy de Maupassant**

Question: Are you choosing the most empowering environment or is the environment choosing you?

Sponsors

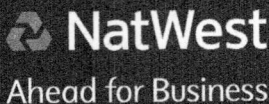

NatWest
Ahead for Business

NatWest

Business Ambitions, we'll support yours all the way.

Whether you're starting a new business or run a multi-million pound enterprise, we want to help you achieve your ambitions.

We believe in providing the best possible breadth and depth of support to you and your business and that's why our team of 3,000 locally based Relationship Managers go through independent accreditation to ensure they fully understand the challenges and opportunities for your business. (Numbers based on RBS Group.)

It's also why we have developed a wide range of products and services that can be tailored to meet your needs – whether it's through specialist financial propositions, unique business planning and management software, or sector and industry information, guides and case studies. And why we provide a network of business service experts who can provide additional support and even outsourcing of your legal and HR requirements.

MINI

Since the first MINI rolled off production lines in 1959, the brand has been synonymous with unrivalled design, nimble agility, and space-saving practicality. Alec Issigonis' inaugural design started from humble beginnings, having been sketched on the back of a napkin, but has become the major player in the success of Plant Oxford's manufacturing history and a triumph of the entire British Motor Industry.

With its rapidly expanding product range, MINI's reputation is constantly being strengthened and has therefore opened up the range as a viable option for the corporate market. The new MINI 5-door Hatch, for example, delivers the same distinctive styling, unrivalled efficiency and go-kart handling as the MINI 3-door Hatch, but with the added benefit of 5 doors, increased leg room and boot space. Also the MINI Countryman, still typically MINI but with added practicality and all round more space, making it an exceptional addition to the range, especially for company car drivers.

As well as delivering impressive economy and performance, MINI's combination of eye-catching design, low running costs and exceptionally strong residual values stack up to make it a company car driver's best friend. Due to the ongoing changes in the market, efficiency has never been more important for business customers and MINI has continued to lead the pack year on year, winning BusinessCar's Supermini of the Year award for 12 consecutive years. Also most recently the MINI Hatch has been awarded Auto Express Car of the Year along with Best Premium Small Car in 2014.

MINI is proud to sponsor the Great British Entrepreneur Awards 2014 and wishes all who have taken part the best in their future.

AXA Business Insurance

AXA Business Insurance specialises in protection for micro, small and medium-sized businesses in the UK. We are proud of the people we protect. After all, entrepreneurs like you are the power at the heart of the UK economy.

Our cover is designed to keep your business running, whatever lies ahead. It's easy to purchase business insurance online at **axa.co.uk/business** Choose from public liability, employers' liability and professional indemnity insurance and tailor it to suit your business – so you only pay for what you need. And if your business needs are more complex, you can call our dedicated advisers on 0845 606 0941.[1]

What's more, with a 97% customer satisfaction score[2] and an award-winning[3] claims service, we're here to get you back on your feet when the going gets tough.

Our approach to insurance means providing free guidance on business risk and protection. For tips and advice visit Business Guardian Angel at **businessguardianangel.com** or follow **@AXABizTeam** on Twitter.

Protection you can rely on

We're part of the AXA Group, a worldwide leader in financial services. We operate across 56 countries with over 157,000 employees and 102 million customers. In the UK alone, AXA Insurance helps around 13 million customers every day.

---

1   Lines are open Monday to Friday, 8am to 8pm, and Saturday, 9am to 2pm. Calls charged at local rate.

2   97% customer satisfaction rating based on 2,024 online reviews. Accurate as of 1 September 2014.

3   Following the 2011 riots in the UK's major cities, we were recognised with a leading industry award for the quality of support we gave to affected businesses (July 2012, British Insurance Awards, Major Losses category).

Croner

Established in 1947, Croner is the UK's leading provider of employment law and health & safety advice, information and software with an extensive suite of products and services designed to help owner-managed businesses manage risk and compliance more efficiently and effectively.

Our services include practical advice and consultancy, pay and benefits, online tools, support for employment tribunal representation and specialist areas such as education and transport.

What makes us special:

- We employ legally qualified people who have relevant professional training who are commercially astute and can translate legal information into practical guidance

- Our employee retention rates are high which means we develop close relationships with our customers

- Croner was the first UK business to launch software enabled solutions in its markets: Croner Simplify launched in 2010

- We have the UK's largest independent pay and benefits databases

- Our litigation service provides a successful resolution in 97% of cases for customers

- Our experts receive 300,000 calls each year to the professional advisory service and the length of these calls are not limited by time

- We are the only company that provides insurance protection which will cover you no matter what happens.

Croner is part of Wolters Kluwer, a global leader in professional information services. In the UK Wolters Kluwer operates under the Croner, CCH and Twinfield brands.

If you would like to find out more about how Croner can support your organisation with employment or safety management, contact us on 01455 897187, email **partnership@wolterskluwer.co.uk** or visit **www. cronersolutions.co.uk.**

Dell

For more than 26 years, Dell has played a critical role in transforming computing, enabling more affordable and more pervasive access to technology around the world. Today, its goals remain the same – bringing innovative solutions to customers, doing right by them and believing in the dreams of entrepreneurs.

Dell develops and delivers innovative technology and services that give its customers the power to do more. Through its technology products and services Dell is committed to helping small and medium businesses grow and better serve their customers by drawing greater value from technology.

= Exact

And it all comes together.

Exact Online

Exact Online is one of Europe's leading suppliers of cloud accounting and business software. We help SMEs look at their numbers and their business in a different way. After all, business isn't just about having ideas; it's about understanding and managing your business in a way that helps turn those ideas into successful ones.

We combine accounting software with the software that's essential to run a business, in one cloud-based system. All the critical performance information is available in real-time on an easy to understand, personalised dashboard. It means businesses can look at their numbers differently by having an holistic view of their business at any given time, and from anywhere. We call it Big Picture Business Software.

At Exact Online, we understand that entrepreneurs are busy enough as it is without having to be a full-time accountant or finance director as well. Which is why we've created a portfolio of software solutions that allow you to collaborate better with those that are, and to give you access to the insights that are needed to make the right business decisions that will keep you ahead of the game.

"We're delighted to be sponsoring the Great British Entrepreneur Awards. It's a chance for us to recognise the fantastic work and talent among UK entrepreneurs," said Lucy Fox, General Manager UK Cloud Solutions at Exact.

"We are proud to be working with and supporting more and more UK entrepreneurs that are shining lights in their field, helping them with the right tools and insights to turn their innovative ideas into the business success stories we can all be proud of."

FedEx

Take Your Business Further, Faster

Here in the UK SMEs make up a staggering 99.9% of all private sector businesses and it's the entrepreneurial skills and innovation of these companies that FedEx wants to help foster and grow.

We do this by providing the e-commerce, business and transportation guidance vital for your continued success. We recognise too that being a new business doesn't necessarily mean you're a small shipper or that the challenges you face are any less daunting.

That's why we make sure you have full access to our range of services designed to help your business operate on the world stage. And we add to this the strategic expertise to make sure every stage of your growth is as smooth and successful as we can make it.

So when you're navigating the intricacies of customs forms, trade regulations, duties, taxes and all the other complications of international shipping, you can be confident that there's someone by your side at all times to help and support you with:

- Unrivalled shipping services from urgent to not-so-urgent

- Specialist expertise to take care of customs and packaging

- Attractive discounts and welcome rewards

- Hassle-free shipping to and from 220 countries and territories worldwide

Get in touch with our dedicated business team today to help grow your business internationally tomorrow. They're keen and eager to help you take advantage of the world of opportunities in front of you. Find out more at **fedex.com/gb** or simply call 08456 07 08 09.

Friendly Pensions

Friendly Pensions is an innovative pension provider specialising in auto enrolment solutions for workplace pensions. Built as a highly efficient, agile and responsive business, Friendly Pensions utilises cutting edge technology and cloud software platforms throughout the organisation to position it firmly at the forefront of the industry. A family run British business with a range of solutions including self-serve cloud payroll, payroll with integrated auto enrolment and a fully managed service. We are a new breed of pension company setting new standards within the pensions arena.

Based at Canada Square, Canary Wharf, Friendly Pensions can be found on the web at: **www.friendly-pensions.com** / **@friendlypension**

KASPERSKY🌐

Kaspersky Lab

Kaspersky Lab is the world's largest privately held vendor of endpoint protection solutions. The company is ranked among the world's top four vendors of security solutions for endpoint users. Throughout its 15-year history Kaspersky Lab has remained an innovator in IT security and provides effective digital security solutions for consumers, SMBs and enterprises. The company currently operates in almost 200 countries and territories across the globe, providing protection for over 300 million users worldwide.

Kingston Smith

Helping clients succeed

Kingston Smith

For the last 90 years Kingston Smith has provided expert accountancy and business advice to entrepreneurial businesses. Today, we remain true to our roots and continue to help our clients achieve their objectives.

Accessibility is an important part of our service. We have six offices in London and the South East: in the City and West End, Heathrow, Redhill, Romford and St Albans. As such we are dedicated to helping and supporting local businesses.

We understand that our clients need an adviser they can rely on, someone they can trust and who will provide a level of service that is quite simply beyond expectation. It's our people's passion and commitment to the success of our clients that makes this possible. Our dedicated experts work with our clients to understand their issues, identify opportunities and solve their problems.

The range of services we provide are extensive. As well as our core audit, accountancy and tax advice, we also provide consultancy, corporate finance, employment, financial planning and insolvency advice.

OKI

OKI Systems

Oki Systems UK is part of Oki Europe, a division of Oki Data Corporation, a global business-to-business organisation dedicated to creating professional in-house printed communications products, applications and services designed to increase the efficiency of today's and tomorrow's businesses. The company is well-established as one of the UK's leading printer brands, in terms of value and units shipped.

Oki Systems UK's award-winning product portfolio comprises seven distinct segments: managed print services, colour and mono printers, multifunctional devices, which combine printing, copying, scanning and faxing functionalities, as well as serial dot matrix printers, faxes and specialty printers for point-of-sales and manufacturing. Its expanding product range has recently won a series of high-profile awards including the Print.IT Editor's Choice Award, the 2012 Go Green award, and the PCPro Laser Printer award.

Oki Data Corporation is a subsidiary of Tokyo-based Oki Electric Industry Co. Ltd., established in 1881 and Japan's first telecommunications manufacturer.

XLN

XLN is one of the fastest growing companies in the UK having already supplied Phone Lines, Broadband, Mobile, Card Processing and Energy to over 250,000 small businesses across every postcode of the UK.

Founded by Christian Nellemann as XLN Telecom in 2002, XLN set out to shake things up. Standing shoulder to shoulder with 1000s of small businesses we use our combined purchasing power to get our customers an excellent deal. We're here to ensure Britain's 'Heroes of the Economy' never pay too much again and always receive the world class service they deserve.

Christian is the UK's only serial entrepreneur to pick up the Ernst & Young Entrepreneur of the Year award twice. As such, he was introduced to Ernst & Young's prestigious Global Hall of Fame, an elite corps of men and women who have been recognized for their exceptional entrepreneurial achievements. He is one of only 13 individuals to be inducted into the Hall of Fame in the last 15 years.

In 2012, XLN was listed as #24 in the Sunday Times Buyout Track 100 and #49 in the Sunday Times Profit Track which lists the private companies with the fastest growing profits. In 2011 XLN won a British Venture Capital Association (BVCA) award for 'Best Private Equity Backed Management Team'. XLN has also been a National Business Awards Finalist for 7 years: 2004, 2005, 2006, 2009, 2010, 2012 & 2013.

More details at: **www.xln.co.uk**

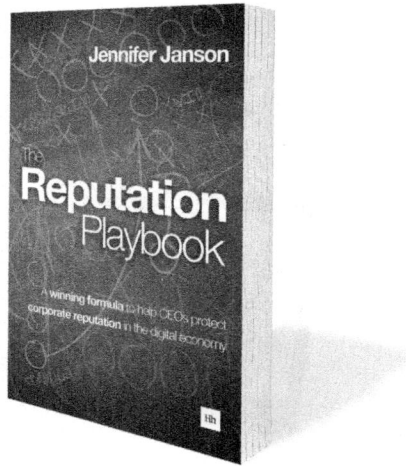

The UK's leading business content partner

Creating bespoke books, eBooks and apps

For businesses big and small

Harriman House is a content producer specialising in business and finance. We publish our own range of print and digital products and also offer our unique high quality services to corporate clients, working with them to produce a range of bespoke content solutions. Get in touch now to find the right solution for you!

SOLUTIONS.HARRIMAN-HOUSE.COM

9 780857 194381